THE NOUVELLE CUISINE

of
Jean and Pierre
Troisgros

THE NOUVELLE CUISINE

of
Jean and Pierre
Troisgros

Edited and adapted by
Caroline Conran

MACMILLAN LONDON

Cuisiniers à Roanne:
Les Recettes originales de Jean et Pierre Troisgros
© Editions Robert Laffont S.A., Paris 1977
(In the collection *'Les recettes originales de... dirigée par Claude Lebey'*.)

This English translation and adaptation
© Macmillan London Ltd 1980

ISBN 0 333 32977 5
THE NOUVELLE CUISINE OF JEAN AND PIERRE TROISGROS
First published 1980 by
MACMILLAN LONDON LIMITED
4 Little Essex Street London WC2R 3LF
and Basingstoke

First published 1982 by
PAPERMAC
a division of Macmillan Publishers Limited
London and Basingstoke

Associated companies in Auckland, Dallas,
Delhi, Dublin, Hong Kong, Johannesburg,
Lagos, Manzini, Melbourne, Nairobi, New York,
Singapore, Tokyo, Washington and
Zaria
Reprinted 1983 (twice)

Translation by Caroline Conran and Fay Sharman
Colour photographs by Didier Blanchat
Line Drawings by Ton van Es, courtesy of
Uniboek b.v./C.A.J. van Dishoek, Holland.

Printed in Hong Kong

Contents

List of Illustrations

Colour plates

Between pages 32 and 33

Oysters with Winkles (*Huîtres chaudes aux bigorneaux*)
Troisgros Salmon Escalopes with Sorrel (*Escalopes de saumon à l'oseille Troisgros*)

Between pages 64 and 65

Duckling with Blackcurrants (*Canette aux baies de cassis*)
Pigeons with Garlic (*Pigeons aux gousses d'ail en chemise*)

Between pages 240 and 241

Coupe-jarret
Le grand dessert Troisgros
Terrine of Vegetables 'Olympe' (*Terrine de légumes 'Olympe'*)

(photography by Didier Blanchat)

The line drawings by Ton van Es show the Troisgros brothers in their restaurant.

Introduction
by
Caroline Conran

Brother chefs and founder-members of the select group of culinary stars who originated the Nouvelle Cuisine, Jean and Pierre Troisgros run the famous three-star 'Les Frères Troisgros' restaurant at Roanne; it is in fact their old family home. They came to live at the Hôtel des Platanes, hidden behind plane trees immediately opposite Roanne Station, in 1930, when they were two and four years old respectively. But although they have kept their roots, and still operate from what was once just a modest little traditional restaurant run by their father and mother, serving neighbours and travellers with good local produce – eels, river fish and simple meat or game dishes, things have changed.

When he first set up at the Hôtel des Platanes, their father had ambitions for the boys, and as they grew up he coached them and encouraged them, fired them with enthusiasm, and took them on his buying trips. Their natures were developed in the warm and pleasant atmosphere of a good, busy bourgeois kitchen. When they were old enough to leave they went to work in a very different atmosphere. They trained, together with Paul Bocuse, at Lucas-Carton in Paris – in the very traditional, very correct, very exacting kitchen of one of the world's most beautiful restaurants (which still serves food in the old style) – and in the early fifties they went to work for the family godfather of the nouvelle cuisine, Fernand Point, whose restaurant, La Pyramide at Vienne, was at the time the Mecca of all serious eaters, and the foundation of all that was most original in French cooking.

They then came home to Roanne, and started their own kitchen. Within two years they had their first star in Michelin, they were awarded their second in 1965 and their third in 1968. They have been improving and expanding ever since.

However, although their brilliance and dedication has taken them to the top of their métier, the two brothers prefer being chefs to being stars. Every recipe in this book is the product of years of real practical experience and hard work in the kitchen. It starts as an idea, based on some particularly good local material such as river perch or snails, or on the quality of the new season's salmon and the excellence of the sorrel from a certain supplier's market-garden. The famous escalope of salmon on a bed of sorrel (*page 122*), now a favourite dish on the menu of restaurants throughout France, was their invention. Each recipe is worked on in the kitchen by the Troisgros frères and their brigade, until it is really fine and beautiful and starts to seem like a dish that can be served in the restaurant. It is then perfected and finally, redolent of the kitchen it came from, it finds its way into the Troisgros repertoire. This is the sort of cooking that people mean when they discuss the merits of the Nouvelle Cuisine.

Incidentally, for those that have been keeping up with the movement, it will come as no surprise to hear that the star-chefs of France are beginning to use the term Nouvelle Cuisine with increasing freedom. They don't want it to become a narrow path, set about with commandments and rules, but prefer it loosely applied to a movement – and every age has its movements in cookery as much as in painting – which allows new developments and imposes no frustrating restrictions. The movement has as its basis a distaste for 'heavy' food and for thick masking sauces based on flour, but this doesn't mean there is a ban on either. Really creative movements are not based on bans, but on changing outlooks and a feeling for what is right for the times and they thrive on originality and informed experimentation.

So Jean and Pierre Troisgros are innovators, and in this book you will find their inspiring recipes, most of them highly original, which will increase your understanding of the Nouvelle Cuisine at its best.

The ingredients of the Nouvelle Cuisine

Good fresh ingredients are of the greatest importance, and a certain delicacy of approach to chopping and slicing is essential. When a recipe says 'finely-chopped' you can be certain that it means the vegetable, or meat, or whatever, should be cut with an extremely sharp knife into the tiniest dice, not just coarsely chopped or hashed up in a food-processor. The same is true of slicing. Try to apply the same finesse to all your work for the best results.

To some people a number of the ingredients favoured by the Trois-gros brothers and by the other chefs of the Nouvelle Cuisine may seem really rather daunting. Freshwater crayfish, baby eels, hibernating snails, small birds, truffles, wood mushrooms, freshwater perch, sea urchins, winkles – rather a trying shopping-list for a cook living in Manchester or Melbourne, you may think, and you are right.

But if you think that they – or passable preserved versions or acceptable local substitutes – don't exist outside France, you are wrong. It is just that people no longer choose or have never learned to eat them. I don't know where we got our often prudish view about what is edible and what is either so offputting or so extravagant as to be offensive. The French, with their cuisine based firmly on excellent ingredients and their keen – often obsessive – interest in the produce of their beautiful and fertile countryside, must show us the way. In Britain for instance, so close to Northern France, there are snails in the hedges, crayfish in the chalk streams, baby eels in the estuaries (especially that of the Severn). Truffles were once plentiful in Savernake Forest and elsewhere, although the truffle-hunter and his hound are now extinct. Ducks and geese are plentiful but are killed kindly and without having to undergo the indignity of being forced to eat their favourite food to make foie gras – though people constantly encourage their family and friends to over-eat. As for wild mushrooms, an Italian friend of mine once picked two hundred kilos of ceps (*boletus edulis*) in a commuter belt near London last summer and sent kilos of them, dried *funghi porcini*, back to Italy, where they were worth a small fortune. Coarse fishermen throw edible freshwater fish in thousands back into their rivers at weekends and the lobsters which thrive off the rocky coasts of Cornwall, Wales and Scotland are exported to France, where fussy French housewives and restaurateurs recognise their excellence. British cookery books of a hundred years ago contain many traditional recipes for these naturally occurring ingredients, and the same is true – though modified by climatic conditions – of the rest of Western Europe.

In other parts of the world, Australia and South Africa for

example, food of equal interest and quality can be found and, with an imaginative eye for similarities of texture and flavour, substituted in the recipes in this and other French cookery books. For instance although Chinese dried mushrooms, such as shiitake and matsutake, are not the same as European wood mushrooms, they can play a similar role in cooking. And while fish varieties vary from continent to continent, local fish which fall into the same category – firm or soft-fleshed, oily or dry – can be found in oceans, rivers and lakes everywhere. Local crustaceans – yabbies or king prawns – can replace écrevisses and local shellfish the mussels and scallops of the Atlantic. The lively flavour of the fermented crème fraîche which is used in France can be imitated by stirring a few drops of lemon juice or, better still, of buttermilk into ordinary fresh cream and leaving it in a warm place for an hour or so. As to the matter of wine, of course château-bottled French wine is wonderful, but the wine-growers of South Africa and Australia produce table-wines quite as good as the everyday wines of France.

Finally, if you find that your substitute ingredients need more or less cooking or seasoning, or that the barely-cooked meat and fish beloved of French chefs is not to your liking, then adapt the recipe intelligently until you are satisfied with the result. Above all, enjoy yourself. The Nouvelle Cuisine, like all cuisines, is a continually evolving art, and you can take part in the process.

Simple Menus for the Home Cook

Scallops with Sauvignon Sauce (page 148)
Beef 'Fleurie' (page 208)
Forézienne Potatoes (page 234)
Tango Oranges (page 259)

*   *   *   *

Salad of Young Spinach Leaves (page 64)
John Dory with Potatoes (page 140)
Walnut Ice-cream (page 262)

*   *   *   *

Cassolette of Freshwater Crayfish
(or Dublin Bay Prawns) (page 76)
Chicken with Chicory (page 154)
Reinette Apple Pudding (page 268)

*   *   *   *

Pea-pod Soup (page 54)
Raw Beef with Digoinaise Sauce (page 205)
Clafoutis with Kiwis (page 264)

*   *   *   *

Boiled Eggs with Small Shrimps (page 113)
Veal Chops with Watercress (page 198)
Tomato Tomatoes (page 242)
Prunes in Dessert Wine with Cream (page 256)

Advanced Menus for the Home Cook

Salad of Hen Pheasants (page 66)
Troisgros Salmon Escalopes with Sorrel (page 122)
Peaches and Almonds in Beaujolais (page 258)

*　　*　　*　　*

Fresh Asparagus with Costelloise Sauce (page 43)
Pigeons with Garlic (page 160)
Mother Carles' Potatoes (page 236)
Rhubarb Tart with Cream (page 270)

*　　*　　*　　*

Almond Soup (page 55)
Saddle of Lamb with Broad Beans (page 192)
Triple-tiered Chocolate Cake (page 276)
Pamélas (page 260)

*　　*　　*　　*

Terrine of Vegetables 'Olympe' (page 100) with
Cold Tomato Sauce 'Jean Yanne' (page 44)
Fillets of Beef with Shallots (page 212)
Praline Soufflé (page 284)

*　　*　　*　　*

Queen Scallop Soup (page 50)
Chicken with Fresh Country Herbs (page 158)
Curly Cucumbers in Cream (page 232)
Opus Incertum (page 280) with Fresh Raspberries

Measurements

Since the introduction of metric measurements in the kitchen in Britain and elsewhere, cookery-book writers have been faced with all sorts of headaches, as it is now necessary to give two different measurements at once.

In this book the usual business of converting pounds and ounces to grammes has been reversed, but the problems remain the same.

The difficulty lies in finding sensible equivalents – one ounce actually equals 28·350 grammes, for example. So to prevent situations where the reader is supposed to measure out 0·353 of an ounce (10 grammes), and so on, we have followed the usual practice of rounding the quantities up or down to the nearest number of ounces or pints.

However, even so, some measurements are distinctly fiddly, so we suggest taking the (eventually) inevitable plunge and obtaining metric scales and measuring jug – you can then use the original measurements.

If this is impossible, use your own judgement as to whether it is important to be exact or not.

Australian Metrication

The recipes in this book were originated in metric measures. The Imperial equivalents given throughout the book follow the British conventions of typography and rounding up and down. In Australia, the Metric Conversion Board recommends different conventions. For example the Australians work to 1 oz = 30 g, whereas the British work to 1 oz = 25 g. The best advice we can give is that you should use metric scales and measures, and only use the Imperial measures as a rough guide.

Conversion Tables

WEIGHT

1. Exact equivalents (to two places of decimals)

Metric	*British*
25 g	0·88 oz
100 g	3·53 oz
1 kg	2·20 lb
British	*Metric*
1 oz	28·35 g
8 oz	226·78 g
1 lb	0·45 kg (453·6 g)
1½ lb	0·68 kg (680·4 g)
2 lb	0·91 kg (907·2 g)

2. Approximate equivalents

Metric	*British*
25 g	1 oz
50 g	1¾–2 oz
75 g	2½ oz
100 g	3½ oz
200 g	7 oz
500 g (0·5 kg)	1 lb 2 oz (18 oz)
1000 g (1 kg)	2¼ lb (36 oz)

LIQUID MEASURES

1. Exact equivalents (to two places of decimals)

Metric	*British*
250 ml (0·25 litres)	0·44 pints
500 ml (0·5 litres)	0·88 pints
1 litre	1·76 pints
British	*Metric*
½ pint	0·28 litres
1 pint	0·57 litres

2. Approximate equivalents

Metric	*British*
150 ml	¼ pint
250 ml	scant half pint
300 ml	½ pint
500 ml (0·5 litres)	scant pint
750 ml	1¼ pints
1000 ml (1 litre)	1¾ pints
1·5 litres	2½ pints
2 litres	3½ pints

OVEN TEMPERATURES

Temperature equivalents for oven thermostat markings

Degrees Fahrenheit (°F)	Gas Regulo Mark	Degrees Centigrade (°C)
225	$\frac{1}{4}$	110
250	$\frac{1}{2}$	130
275	1	140
300	2	150
325	3	170
350	4	180
375	5	190
400	6	200
425	7	220
450	8	230
475	9	240
500	10	250

Authors'
Foreword

Our father, Jean-Baptiste Troisgros, always said that cooking should be a carefully balanced reflection of all the good things of the earth. Although he was not a trained chef, and could only make up for this by encouraging his children to pursue the vocation that he himself never had, he had an instinctive feeling for cooking and instilled in us many of his ideas, which at the time were quite revolutionary.

He didn't like the basic stocks and glazes which were used in every dish in all the grand restaurants and he made us do without them as well as dispensing with all the flour-based sauces. He didn't like recipes that were finished off at the table by the waiters – he thought the chef should be responsible for his dishes right up to the last moment. He didn't approve of complex presentation, hence his idea of serving each course on its own large plate – a practice which we were the first to use. Most of all he disliked the traditional garnishes, the single steamed potato, the tomato, the watercress or the large croûton, which cluttered up the plate without adding anything to the dish.

On the other hand, he did love good ingredients ... and so do we. We get our snails from the schoolboys of Roanne, the small market gardeners of our region provide us with the best of their vegetables, and our salmon are brought to us by the fishermen of the Allier. Our lobsters come from Brittany and our chickens from Bresse. Like careful housewives we do our own marketing every morning and we only buy produce that is in season and of irreproachably high quality and absolute freshness.

We respect the good things of the earth that our father spoke about. Why ruin and cover up the taste of a good piece of meat, the fine flavour of a fish or shellfish, and the springlike freshness of tiny young vegetables? Cook them with great care, accompany them with delicate austere sauces, but let the ingredients speak for themselves: this is what we are trying to do.

As it becomes simpler and lighter the chef's art is getting nearer to the home cook's art, and this is what we have set out to show in this book.

JEAN AND PIERRE TROISGROS

Basic Recipes

Stocks for the Home Cook

Les fonds à l'usage des ménagères

Stock has a bad reputation now but it still plays a vital part in the elaborate sauces of French cookery. Here we give recipes for dark and light stocks and for fish fumet. We have deliberately cut down on highly complicated recipes which the housewife would find difficult and time-consuming. We very seldom use roux for thickening, much preferring the processes of reduction and liaison with butter.

In the old days, stock would be made the day before it was needed or even on the same day. But now, with a freezer, you can prepare it once or twice a month (or more often), depending on your requirements. It can be frozen in small containers – yoghourt pots or plastic boxes – and these should, if possible, be hermetically sealed. We recommend that you mark the type of stock and the date of freezing on the container. The proportions we give in the recipes are small, but you can always increase them if you want to keep a supply.

We know that cooks are often put off by the idea of stocks and glazes, but there are alternatives. You can use the broth from a pot-au-feu, or the cooking liquid from a poached chicken; even the commercial meat extracts and fish stocks can be improved by the clever use of herbs and flavourings – tomatoes, mushroom stalks and peelings, a bouquet garni, crushed peppercorns.

Light Poultry Stock

Fond blanc de volaille

For 2·25 litres (4 pints) stock
Cooking time: 45 minutes from the time it comes
to the boil

Ingredients   1 kg ($2\frac{1}{4}$ lb) poultry carcases and necks
60 g (2 oz) carrots
50 g ($1\frac{3}{4}$ oz) onions
the white part of a leek
half a stick of celery
2 cloves of garlic
a clove
1 heaped teaspoon coarsely-crushed black
    peppercorns

1   Put the poultry bones and trimmings in a large saucepan, fill it almost to the top with cold water, bring to the boil and skim.

2   Add the vegetables and seasoning and make certain that it stays at a rolling boil for 45 minutes. Skim off the fat with a ladle as it rises to the surface (these two points are important if you want to achieve a crystal-clear stock).

3   Strain the stock through a conical strainer.

* For a more full-bodied stock, cook a whole boiling fowl or a knuckle of veal in with the stock. These can be used afterwards for another recipe.

Editor's note   If you can obtain poultry feet as well as the bones and necks, these make a very good contribution to a poultry stock; prepare them by blanching them for 5 minutes in boiling water and then peeling off the outer scales and removing the claws. They are then ready to be added to the stock.

Dark Veal Stock

Fond de veau brun

For 1 litre ($1\frac{3}{4}$ pints) stock
Cooking time: 2 to 4 hours from the time it comes
   to the boil

Ingredients   1 kg ($2\frac{1}{4}$ lb) veal bones, chopped into pieces by the
                 butcher
               100 g ($3\frac{1}{2}$ oz) carrots
               50 g ($1\frac{3}{4}$ oz) sliced onions
               a clove of garlic
               a bouquet garni

1   Put the bones in a roasting tin and brown them in a hot oven.

2   Put the bones into a large saucepan with the vegetables, garlic
and herbs. Do not add any salt. Almost fill the pan with water, bring
to the boil and skim.

3   Boil gently but steadily for 2 to 4 hours. Skim frequently and
add cold water when necessary to keep the bones covered. At the
end of the cooking, the stock should be reduced to 1 litre ($1\frac{3}{4}$ pints).

4   Strain through a conical strainer.

Tomato-flavoured Demi-glace

Demi-glace tomatée

For half a litre (scant pint) demi-glace
Cooking time: 1 hour from the time it starts to boil

Ingredients 1 litre (1¾ pints) dark veal stock (page 28)
½ tablespoon tomato purée
3 fresh tomatoes, coarsely chopped
half a carrot, ⎱
half an onion, ⎰ cut into mirepoix dice
a stick of celery
some parsley stalks
5 coarsely-crushed black peppercorns
1 tablespoon arachide oil

1 Sweat the carrot and the onion gently in the oil in a covered saucepan. Add the tomatoes and tomato purée, the stick of celery, the parsley stalks and the stock.

2 Let it simmer over a low heat for about an hour, skimming from time to time. Add cold water if necessary – there should be 500 ml (scant pint) liquid left after reducing. Ten minutes before the end of the cooking time, add the crushed peppercorns.

3 Strain through a fine conical strainer and keep until required.

* Demi-glace is a dark stock which has been reduced and flavoured.

Editor's note Whenever appropriate the Troisgros prefer to use this tomato-flavoured demi-glace because it has an interesting flavour.

Meat Glaze

Glace de viande

This is made by reducing a dark veal stock
Cooking time: this varies with the speed of the
reducing, so it is impossible to give a precise time

Ingredients   4 litres (7 pints), at least, veal stock (page 28)

1   Reduce the stock over a low heat. With a ladle carefully remove any scum which forms round the edge of the saucepan. The clarity of the stock depends on this being done carefully.

2   When the stock is greatly reduced, transfer the liquid to a smaller saucepan. It must reduce by nine tenths altogether and the resulting glaze should be crystal clear, glistening, and syrupy.

* Meat glaze can be used in the making of steak au poivre and to give body to sauces.

Game Stock

Fond de gibier

For 1 litre (1¾ pints) stock
Cooking time: 3 hours from the time it comes to
the boil

Ingredients   1 kg (2¼ lb) carcases or giblets of feathered game
and trimmings of furred game
1 litre (1¾ pints) red wine
500 ml (scant pint) veal demi-glace (page 29)
2½ tablespoons arachide oil
a carrot, finely chopped
an onion, finely chopped
a bouquet garni

1   Brown the carcases, giblets and trimmings in the oil in a saucepan
for 10 minutes. Add the carrot and onion and brown them lightly.
Then add the red wine and the demi-glace.

2   Bring to the boil and simmer very gently for 3 hours, skimming
frequently and adding cold water to maintain the level of liquid. You
should end up with 1 litre (1¾ pints) stock.

3   Strain through a fine conical strainer, skim off any remaining
fat and keep in a cool place until required.

Fish Fumet

Fumet de poisson

For about 1 litre (1¾ pints) fumet
Cooking time: about 35 minutes

Ingredients   1 kg (2¼ lb) fish heads and bones – preferably sole,
turbot, conger eel, whiting and/or rascasse
100 g (3½ oz) onions, sliced
a bouquet garni

1   Sweat the fish and the onions gently, without fat, in a large un-covered saucepan, for about 10 minutes. Just cover the bones with cold water, add the bouquet garni and bring to the boil. Remove the scum which forms on the surface and simmer over a gentle heat for 25 minutes.

2   Strain through a fine conical strainer and keep in the refrigerator until required for use.

* The stock will set to a jelly when cold, so it is a good idea to pour it into special containers while still warm, ready for freezing.

* The court-bouillon opposite can be used in two ways. First, as it is, for cooking fish. Or second, for poaching shellfish, using the poached and drained vegetables, moistened with dry white wine (pre-ferably Sancerre) and blended with butter over a high flame, to make a delicious sauce for freshwater crayfish tails, Dublin Bay prawns or scallops (see page 76).

Oysters with Winkles – *Huîtres chaudes aux bigorneaux* (page 88)

Troisgros Salmon Escalopes with Sorrel – *Escalopes de saumon à l'oseille Troisgros* (page 122)

Court-bouillon for Fish and Shellfish

Nage pour poissons, crustacés ou coquillages

Preparation time: 30 minutes
Cooking time: 6 minutes

Ingredients

400 g (14 oz) carrots
150 g (5¼ oz) sticks of celery
250 g (8¾ oz) button onions
40 g (1½ oz) shallots
a whole head of garlic
a sprig of thyme
a bayleaf
a leaf of sage
a sprig of tarragon
10 parsley stalks
the green part of a leek
a quarter of a red chilli pepper
5 white peppercorns
3 coriander seeds
2 star anise
2 cloves
25 g (1 oz) salt
3 litres (5¼ pints) water

1 First prepare the vegetables and herbs. Remove the strings from the stick of celery and cut it in half lengthwise. Then cut the celery and carrots into julienne strips 5 cm (2 in) long. Slice the onions and shallots into rings. Prick the head of garlic here and there with the tip of a knife blade. Make a bunch with the thyme, bayleaf, sage and tarragon, wrap it in a piece of leek and tie into a bundle with a piece of cotton. Cut the red pepper into julienne strips and the parsley stalks into pieces 2 cm (¾ in) long. Lightly crush the peppercorns and enclose them in a little muslin bag with the cloves, star anise and coriander.

2 Put all the ingredients into a saucepan. Cover to the top with cold water, add the salt and bring to the boil. Cook for 4 minutes.

Pastries

Yeast Pastry

Pâte à foncer fine

For eight people
Preparation time: 15 minutes

Ingredients   250 g (8¾ oz) flour
150 g (5¼ oz) softened butter
2 egg yolks
150 ml (¼ pint) lukewarm milk
6 g fresh yeast (a piece the size of a walnut)
25 g (1 oz) icing sugar
a pinch of salt

1   Spread the flour in a ring on a board or worktop leaving a well in the centre. Put the salt, sugar, lukewarm milk and the yeast into the middle. Make sure they are all dissolved by stirring and mixing them with your fingertips inside the well of flour.

2   Add the egg yolks and the softened butter, draw the flour gradually into the well and work everything together, still using your fingertips.

3   Work it lightly to a smooth dough, without handling it too much.

4   When it is ready, make it into a ball and put it into a large bowl. Cover with a plate and keep in a cool place.

Sweet Flan Pastry

Pâte sucrée

For eight people
Preparation time: 15 minutes

Ingredients 250 g (8¾ oz) flour
90 g (3 oz) softened butter
4 egg yolks
125 g (4¼ oz) sugar
a pinch of salt
½ tablespoon water

---

1   Spread the flour in a ring on a board or worktop, leaving a well in the centre. Put the butter, sugar and salt in the hollow and work them together, then add the egg yolks, beaten with a few drops of water, half at a time.

2   Gradually incorporate the flour and smear the pastry into a thin layer across the board, spreading it with the palm of your hand. Scrape it together with a spatula and repeat this spreading and mixing process once more.

3   Scrape the pastry together again, form it into a ball and put it into a polythene bag. Keep it in a cool place until it is needed.

Flaky Pastry

Pâte feuilletée

Preparation time: 1 hour 30 minutes

Ingredients 500 g (18 oz) flour
500 g (18 oz) butter
15 g ($\frac{1}{2}$ oz) salt
200 ml ($\frac{1}{3}$ pint) water

The basic pastry

1 Sprinkle the flour in a ring on your worktop leaving a well in the centre. Put the salt and the water in the middle. With your right hand, work in the flour, drawing it gradually round the inner edges into the well. This operation should be done quickly, without kneading, to keep the dough light. The basic pastry is ready when all the flour has been incorporated.

2 Scrape the pastry from the work-surface with a spatula, form it into a ball and put it on a plate. Make a few parallel cuts across it with a knife so that the air penetrates and the pastry loses its elasticity. Chill in the refrigerator for 20 minutes.

The butter

3 Place the butter between two sheets of plastic film and beat it with the rolling-pin to obtain a smooth but firm consistency. It should end up like a sort of thin very supple rectangular cake.

4 Put the basic pastry in front of you and roll it out into a rectangle 3 cm ($1\frac{1}{4}$ in) thick.

5 Place the butter in the centre of the rectangle and fold over the four sides of the pastry so that they meet in the middle, and the butter is completely enclosed.

6 Lightly flour the work-surface and roll out the pastry into an even rectangle about 6 cm (2½ in) thick. The pastry is now ready for its six 'folds'.

Folding the pastry

7 Folding means that the pastry is first rolled out into a strip and then folded over. Keep your hands flat on the rolling-pin and always roll in one direction. Starting in the middle of the rectangle, roll out the pastry away from you to half its thickness. Then return the rolling-pin to the middle (in order not to go over the same ground again) and roll it back towards you. The pastry should now be 2 cm (¾ in) thick. Fold it over in three like an envelope. At this stage, with the first fold complete, the pastry is known as 'pâton'.

8 You are now ready to start the second fold. Turn the pastry round through 90° to the right and proceed as for the first fold. Then cover the 'pâton' with a damp cloth to prevent it drying out and let it rest for 20 minutes in the refrigerator.

9 Give the pastry two further folds, as described above.

10 A few moments before the pastry is required, give it two final folds (the fifth and sixth). The flaky pastry is now ready.

* A marble table or working top is best for making flaky pastry – particularly in summer when it is most important to keep the pastry cool.

Editor's note   Failing a marble top you can cool down any wooden or formica working surface by leaving a large polythene bag filled with ice-cubes on the surface for 10–15 minutes, before you start working the pastry.
This recipe makes a considerable quantity of pastry, enough for about twenty large tarts. It freezes well.

Choux Pastry

Pâte à choux

For eight sweet éclairs or puffs
Preparation time: 15 minutes

Ingredients   60 g (2 oz) butter
125 g (4¼ oz) flour
4 eggs
12 g (level tablespoon) sugar
2·5 g (scant teaspoon) salt
250 ml (scant half pint) water

1   Pour the water into a saucepan, add the salt and sugar and the butter cut into small pieces. Bring to the boil and, as soon as the butter has melted, add the flour all at once.

2   Work the dough over a moderate heat with a wooden spatula to dry it out a little. After about a minute the mixture should come away from the sides of the saucepan.

3   Remove the pan from the heat and incorporate the eggs, one at a time, mixing them in with the spatula. The pastry should now be smooth and sticky.

4   Transfer the mixture to a stainless steel bowl. It is now ready for use.

* The pastry can be kept for several days in a cool place, covered with aluminium foil.

Editor's note   If making choux pastry for Poached Eggs 'Bodin' (page 108), omit the sugar.

Sauces

Fresh Tomato Sauce

Coulis de tomates

For four people
Preparation time: 25 minutes
Cooking time: 35 minutes

Ingredients 1 kg (2¼ lb) tomatoes
half an onion
2 cloves of garlic, unpeeled
a bouquet garni
60 g (2 oz) butter
salt, freshly-ground pepper
a pinch of sugar

1 Plunge the tomatoes in boiling water for a moment, skin them and cut them in half. Press each half in your hand to squeeze out the seeds and excess juice, then cut the tomato flesh into small dice. Chop the onion.

2 Put half the butter – 30 g (1 oz) – into a sauté pan and sweat the onion gently for 5 minutes without browning. Add the tomatoes, the two unpeeled cloves of garlic and the bouquet garni. Season with salt, pepper and a pinch of sugar, cover the pan and cook over a medium heat for about 30 minutes.

3 Remove the garlic and the bouquet garni and sieve the tomatoes in a mouli-légumes, or purée in a liquidiser or food processor and then sieve. Return the sauce to the pan, bring to the boil again and then transfer it to a bowl.

4 Before using the sauce, bring it to the boil once more and stir in the remaining 30 g (1 oz) butter. Taste for seasoning.

Cold Sauce for Shellfish Salads

Sauce froide pour crustacés

For four people
Preparation time: 20 minutes
Cooking time: 20 minutes

Ingredients   *for the stock*
the heads of 20 freshwater crayfish or Dublin
    Bay prawns **or** 20 small crabs
1 tablespoon cognac
1½ tablespoons dry white wine
1 tablespoon arachide oil
200 ml (⅓ pint) fish fumet (page 32)
2 teaspoons tomato purée

for the sauce
150 ml (¼ pint) whipping cream
1 tablespoon wine vinegar
1 teaspoon Dijon mustard
a pinch of paprika
8 fresh tarragon leaves, chopped
a sprig of parsley, coarsely chopped
salt, freshly-ground pepper

1   Crush the shellfish or crabs in a liquidiser or food processor.
Sauté them in the hot oil in a saucepan for 5 minutes, stirring all
the time. Deglaze with the cognac, add the white wine and then the
fish fumet, and salt. Stir in the tomato purée and simmer for 20
minutes.

2   Strain the stock through a conical strainer, pressing the shells
firmly with a spoon or the back of a ladle. Return to the pan and
reduce until there are about 4 tablespoons liquid left. Allow to cool
and then chill in the refrigerator.

3   Mix the mustard, cream, vinegar, paprika, salt and pepper in a
mixing bowl. Whisk for a few moments gradually incorporating the
shellfish stock. Then add the parsley and tarragon.

Editor's note   The crabs used in this recipe are small swimming crabs
or 'étrilles', the sort caught in rock pools and estuaries by small boys.

Sauce 'Albert Prost'

Sauce Albert Prost

For four people
Preparation time: 20 minutes
Cooking time: 10 minutes

Ingredients   1 bulb of Florence fennel together with its leaves
2 shallots
40 g (1½ oz) parsley
250 ml (scant half pint) double cream
20 g (¾ oz) butter
1 tablespoon dry white wine
1 tablespoon fresh lemon juice
salt, freshly-ground pepper

1   Trim the fennel. Weigh out 100 g (3½ oz) of the central heart and cut it into large mirepoix dice. Chop the young green leaves from the fennel together with the parsley until you have a fine, moist, green purée, and squeeze in a napkin to extract the juice, which should be set aside in a bowl.

2   Chop the shallots and soften them in the butter in a small heavy pan. Add the diced fennel, cover the pan and cook gently for 7–8 minutes. Deglaze the pan with the white wine and then reduce to a few tablespoons.

3   Add the cream, bring it to the boil and season with a little salt. Allow to boil for a few minutes until you have a light smooth sauce. Then add the fennel and parsley juice, which will turn the sauce a beautiful pistachio-green colour.

4   Taste for seasoning, adding the lemon juice, a generous turn of the peppermill and, if necessary, a pinch of salt.

Editor's note   Albert Prost, one of the Troisgros' best clients at their restaurant, tries out and advises on their new creations.

Digoinaise Mustard Sauce

Sauce Digoinaise

For four people
Preparation time: 25 minutes

Ingredients
2 egg yolks
1 teaspoon Dijon mustard
2½ tablespoons lemon juice
180 ml (scant ⅓ pint) arachide oil
1 shallot, finely chopped
6 drops of Tabasco, salt
2 tablespoons shredded watercress

1 Put the egg yolks, the mustard, a third of the lemon juice and the salt into a large deep mixing bowl. Using a whisk mix them together and then incorporate the oil drop by drop, whisking vigorously (as if you were making mayonnaise). Add the remaining lemon juice at the same time to make the sauce rather liquid, and, if it is still too thick, thin with a few drops of water.

2 Add the chopped shallot, Tabasco and the finely shredded watercress to complete the seasoning.

* This sauce can accompany cold or raw beef. It is also very good with grilled steak and can be used to make céleri rémoulade. The classic céleri rémoulade is celeriac cut into the thinnest shreds on a mandoline or coarsely grated on a grater, blanched for barely a moment in boiling salted water (or sometimes served raw) and mixed with a mustardy mayonnaise.

Editor's note This sauce takes its name from Digoin, near Roanne, where the plates used in the Troisgros' restaurant are made (see the illustration of the coupe-jarret opposite page 224).

Costelloise Sauce

Sauce Costelloise

For four people
Preparation time: 15 minutes
Cooking time: 5 minutes

Ingredients 150 ml ($\frac{1}{4}$ pint) arachide oil
4 tablespoons walnut oil
150 ml ($\frac{1}{4}$ pint) olive oil
2 strips of orange peel
4 tablespoons white wine vinegar
8 white peppercorns, coarsely crushed
   (mignonette pepper)
3 egg yolks
salt

1 Put the three different oils in a saucepan, stir them together and let them get lukewarm on the side of the stove.

2 Chop the orange peel very finely, blanch for 5 minutes in a generous quantity of boiling water, refresh under cold running water and drain in a sieve.

3 Put the vinegar and the mignonette pepper in a saucepan, preferably of tinned copper, and reduce until all but evaporated. Remove the pan from the heat and add 3 tablespoons cold water and then the egg yolks.

4 Place the pan over a very low heat and whisk for about 3 minutes, gradually incorporating the oil in a thin trickle. Add the blanched orange peel and salt lightly. If you have to prepare the sauce in advance, keep it warm in a bain-marie at 45° C/113° F.

Editor's note This sauce may be used to accompany poached fish, hot or cold, and instead of Hollandaise with asparagus or Béarnaise with grilled meat.
Le Côteau lies on the right bank of the Loire opposite Roanne. Its inhabitants, among them Pierre Troisgros, are known as the Costellois.

Cold Tomato Sauce 'Jean Yanne'

Sauce froide à la tomate pour Jean Yanne

For four people
Preparation time: 15 minutes

Ingredients
500 g (18 oz) tomatoes
1 teaspoon tomato purée
1 tablespoon wine vinegar
3 tablespoons virgin olive oil
12 leaves of tarragon, coarsely chopped
a sprig of flat leaved or 'continental' parsley,
   coarsely chopped
$\frac{1}{2}$ teaspoon salt
a pinch of pepper

1   Plunge the tomatoes in boiling water for a moment, skin them and cut them in half. Squeeze each half in your hand to press out the pips and excess juice. Work the remaining pulp into a bowl through a fine sieve, pressing it through with the back of a spoon. Chill until needed.

2   The final stage must be done at the last moment to prevent the oil getting too cold and congealing. Add the tomato purée to the pulp in the bowl, whisking them together thoroughly. Then incorporate the vinegar and the olive oil drop by drop, still whisking. Season with salt and pepper, and stir in the coarsely chopped parsley and tarragon.

* This sauce should be served very cool and can be used to accompany vegetables or fish terrines such as Terrine of Vegetables 'Olympe' (page 100).

* Choose tomatoes that are very ripe and freshly picked.

Editor's note   Virgin olive oil is oil obtained from the first cold pressing of the olives, (they may then be pressed again, with hot or cold rollers, to obtain more but inferior oil); it has the finest, freshest and fruitiest flavour of all olive oils.
The best tomatoes for this sauce are the large irregular Mediterranean tomatoes and should be as red as possible. Hot-house tomatoes can be rather anaemic and tasteless.
Jean Yanne is a film director and friend of the Troisgros brothers.

Tarragon Sauce

Sauce purée d'estragon

For four people
Preparation time: 10 minutes
Cooking time: 8 minutes

Ingredients   160 g (6 oz) spinach
50 g (1¾ oz) freshly-picked tarragon leaves
200 ml (⅓ pint) poultry stock (page 27)
30 crushed white peppercorns
30 g (1 oz) butter
salt

1   Trim and wash the spinach, removing stalks and ribs. Throw it into a saucepan of boiling salted water, and cook, uncovered, for about 4 minutes, and plunge immediately into cold water. Drain.

2   Put the leaves of the tarragon in a sieve and dip into boiling salted water for 1 minute. Refresh under cold water, and drain.

3   Bring the stock to the boil in a small saucepan. Add the crushed pepper and then the tarragon and boil rapidly, uncovered, until it is almost completely evaporated. Add the spinach and heat through.

4   Turn the whole lot into a fine sieve placed over a small saucepan and work it through with a wooden spatula, scraping the sieve thoroughly with the back of a knife.

5   Heat the butter in a frying-pan until it is the colour of hazelnuts (beurre noisette) and incorporate with the purée, whisking it in thoroughly. Keep the sauce warm until required, but don't let it boil.

* This sauce goes particularly well with white meats such as veal and chicken and with eggs.

Soups

Grouse Soup

Crème de grouses

For four people
Preparation time: 1 hour 30 minutes
Cooking time: 40 minutes

Ingredients

3 grouse
1 tablespoon olive oil
half a carrot
1 shallot
25 g (1 oz) rice
a slice of white bread (1·5 cm [¾ in] thick)
50 g (1¾ oz) butter
300 ml (½ pint) double cream
a bouquet garni
6 crushed juniper berries
1 litre (1¾ pints) poultry stock (page 27)
salt, freshly-ground pepper

Editor's note   In the original French version, this recipe was made with eight small fresh thrushes, which, according to Pierre Troisgros, taste very much like grouse.

Preparation

1 Remove the two breasts from the grouse and cut into thin strips. Marinate these in the olive oil, seasoned with salt and pepper, while you prepare the soup.

2 Cut the carrot into fine mirepoix dice and chop the shallot.

3 Put the rice in a sieve and wash under plenty of running water to remove the starch.

4 Cut the bread into 1·5 cm ($\frac{3}{4}$ in) cubes and fry them in 20 g ($\frac{3}{4}$ oz) butter. Keep them hot.

Cooking

5 Brown the grouse carcases rapidly in 20 g ($\frac{3}{4}$ oz) butter in a saucepan. After 10 minutes add the carrot mirepoix and the chopped shallot, cover the pan and sweat for 5 minutes. Add the rice, the bouquet garni, the juniper berries and the stock and simmer for 40 minutes.

6 Remove the carcases and vegetables with a ladle and blend in a liquidiser or food processor. Return to the pan and strain everything through a cloth, or a very fine sauce strainer. Return the soup to the saucepan, add the cream, bring to the boil and taste for seasoning.

7 Drain the strips of breast meat and sauté very briskly in 10 g ($\frac{1}{4}$ oz) butter in a frying-pan for 20 seconds.

Serving

8 Pour the hot soup into a heated soup tureen and serve the grouse fillets and the croûtons separately.

Queen Scallop Soup

Crème de pétoncles

For four people
Preparation time: 45 minutes
Cooking time: 10 minutes

Ingredients

1 kg (2¼ lb) small live Queen scallops in their shells (see note)
5 tablespoons dry white wine
200 ml (⅓ pint) fish fumet (page 32)
a chopped shallot
a sprig of thyme
2 egg yolks
200 ml (⅓ pint) double cream
20 g (¾ oz) butter
20 chives
salt, freshly-ground pepper

1   Wash the scallops quickly without letting them soak in the water. Put them into a fairly large saucepan, add the white wine, fish fumet, chopped shallot, thyme and a pinch of sea salt. Cover the pan hermetically and place over a brisk heat. After 3 minutes, shake the pan so that the scallops on top get to the bottom, and cook for a further 2 minutes.

2   Allow the scallops to cool a little before shelling. The shells will have opened during cooking, so you can now take out the white part, using a knife to detach it from the hollow shell, the flat shell having been detached during cooking. Cut away the gills – usually black – from the edge of the shell, reserving just the white part and the coral. Strain the cooking liquid through a cloth.

3   Beat the egg yolks in a cup with a fork and whisk in 4 tablespoons of the scallop stock; season with a turn of the peppermill.

4   Bring the cream to the boil in a saucepan and, when very much reduced, add the rest of the scallop stock and simmer for 3 or 4 minutes.

5   Remove the pan from the heat and gradually add the egg yolk liaison, stirring all the time with a wooden spoon. Stir in the butter in little pieces. The soup should have the consistency of a very light cream.

6   Chop the chives and put in a warmed soup tureen together with the shelled scallops. Pour the soup over the top and serve.

* Instead of Queen scallops, you can use mussels or, better, eight large scallops cut in four.

Editor's note   Queen scallops are tiny and delicate – if using ordinary large scallops do not attempt to cook them in their shells as they often contain large amounts of sand. Shell them and clean them raw over a bowl, straining any juices that you collect. Wash them thoroughly, rejecting the frilly gills that surround them.

Flageolet Bean Soup with Chicken Livers

Potage de flageolets aux foies de volaille

For four people
Preparation time: 30 minutes
Cooking time: 1 hour

Ingredients 160 g (5½ oz) dried flageolet beans or 350 g
    (12½ oz) fresh flageolet beans in their pods
10 pale fresh chicken livers
3 leeks
3 slices of day-old bread 6 mm (¼ in) thick
65 g (2¼ oz) butter
1½ litres (2½ pints) poultry stock (page 27)
5 tablespoons single cream
salt, freshly-ground pepper

Preparation

1 If using dried flageolet beans, soak for 2 hours or more in warm water and then simmer gently for 2 hours. If using fresh beans, shell them and cook in boiling salted water, uncovered, for 25 minutes.

2 Divide the chicken livers in two and cut out any green parts which have been in contact with the gall bladder. Set 3 livers aside and cut these into small dice 1 cm ($\frac{1}{2}$ in) square.

3 Clean and trim the leeks and slice the white parts thinly.

4 Slice off the crusts and cut the slices of bread into small cubes of 6 mm ($\frac{1}{4}$ in). Fry in 15 g ($\frac{1}{2}$ oz) butter until crisp and golden. Keep them hot.

Cooking

5 In a deep, heavy saucepan, soften the leeks with 30 g (1 oz) butter, add the halved livers and sauté them in the butter for about 10 minutes until they are firm. Add the stock, cover the pan and simmer gently for 25 minutes.

6 Cut two dozen flageolet beans in half lengthwise, and keep them on one side. Add the rest of the beans to the soup. Then sieve in the mouli-légumes or blend in the liquidiser. Return the soup to the pan, add the cream and bring to the boil.

7 Sauté the diced chicken livers in 10 g ($\frac{1}{3}$ oz) butter in a frying-pan for 2 minutes and season with salt and pepper. Whisk the remaining butter into the soup (off the heat) and taste for seasoning.

Serving

8 Put the hot diced chicken livers and the halved beans in the bottom of a soup tureen and pour on the soup through a fine conical strainer. The croûtons should be served separately and floated on the soup at the last moment so that they remain crisp.

Pea-pod Soup

Potage aux cosses de petits pois

For four people
Preparation time: 30 minutes
Cooking time: 1 hour

Ingredients	500 g (1 lb 2 oz) peas in their pods
	4 leeks
	100 g (3½ oz) butter
	a bouquet garni
	the heart of a lettuce
	5 tablespoons double cream
	salt, a little sugar

1   Choose fresh young peas, picked the same day and the sweeter the better. Shell the peas just before making the soup and reserve the pods. Cook the peas rapidly in boiling salted water for 4 to 5 minutes and refresh quickly under cold running water (this is called à l'anglaise).

2   Clean and trim the leeks, chop them coarsely and sweat in 50 g (1¾ oz) butter for 15 minutes in a deep saucepan. Add the pods and 1 litre (1¾ pints) water. Add the bouquet garni, season with salt, cover the pan and simmer for one hour.

3   Take 4 leaves of the lettuce heart and shred them finely into ribbons. Using a pestle, press the contents of the pan through a sieve into a bowl until there is nothing left in the sieve but strings and membranes. Return to the pan and bring back to the boil, stirring with a whisk.

4   Add the cream and bring back to the boil, then remove the saucepan from the heat and incorporate the remaining butter – 50 g (1¾ oz) – shaking the pan to blend it into the soup. Finally, add the peas and taste for seasoning, adding a little sugar if necessary (depending on the peas).

Almond Soup

Soupe aux amandes

For four people
Preparation time: 30 minutes
Cooking time: 5 minutes

Ingredients 200 g (7 oz) shelled almonds, fresh or dried
5 eggs
1 litre (1¾ pints) poultry stock (page 27)
750 ml (1¼ pints) double cream
salt, pepper

1 Cook the eggs in boiling water for 9 minutes, cool under cold running water, peel off their shells and then separate the yolks from the whites. Plunge the almonds into boiling water for a moment and skin.

2 Put the almonds and the egg yolks in a liquidiser or food processor and blend to a smooth paste.

3 Heat the stock in a saucepan, until it is lukewarm, mix in the cream and then gradually incorporate the almond/egg yolk mixture. Stirring constantly with a wooden spatula, bring the soup to the boil. Cook gently for 5 minutes, taste for seasoning and serve very hot.

Carp Soup

Soupe de carpes

For four people
Preparation time: 30 minutes
Cooking time: 1 hour 10 minutes

Ingredients

1 carp weighing 1·5 kg (3 lb 6 oz)
an onion
a bouquet garni
2 cloves of garlic
500 g (1 lb 2 oz) spinach
400 g (14 oz) sorrel
200 g (7 oz) parsley
100 g (3½ oz) chervil
10 leaves of tarragon
100 g (3½ oz) watercress
thyme, bayleaf
50 g (1¾ oz) butter
5 tablespoons double cream
flour and oil for frying
salt, pepper

Preparation

1 Clean and gut the carp, remove the fillet from each side and skin them. Cut off the two parts on the lower half which are flat and boneless, and cut into small slices of about 3 cm (1 in) diameter.

2 For the fumet, break up the head and backbone of the fish with a large knife. Put them, together with trimmings and skin, into a small saucepan with the onion, the bouquet garni, the garlic, 3 litres (5¼ pints) water and a pinch of sea salt. Bring to the boil, skim and simmer gently for 25 minutes. Then strain through a fine conical strainer.

3 Prepare the vegetables and herbs (the spinach, sorrel, parsley, chervil, tarragon and watercress). Remove the tough stalks and veins, wash and drain, and shred them into ribbons to reduce the volume.

Cooking

4 Put the fillets of carp and shredded herbs together with the thyme and bayleaf and butter into a large saucepan, cover and leave to sweat over a low heat for about 15 minutes. Pour in the fumet, bring to the boil, cover and simmer for 40 minutes on a moderate heat.

5 When it is cooked sieve the soup through a mouli-légumes and then strain through a fine sieve. Return to the saucepan, add the cream and bring to the boil. Taste for seasoning, and keep hot.

6 Two minutes before serving the soup, flour the little slices of fish, put them into a frying basket and plunge into very hot oil for no more than 2 minutes, so that they turn golden almost immediately. Drain on kitchen paper and sprinkle with salt.

Serving

7 Serve the soup very hot and offer the fried fish separately on small plates.

Lobster Soup with Elvers

Soupe de homards et de civelles

For four people
Preparation time: 1 hour
Cooking time: 30 minutes

Ingredients 1·6 kg (3 lb 9 oz) live lobsters (2 or 3 small ones)
1 onion
1 shallot
1 carrot
80 g (2¾ oz) elvers (tiny baby eel fry)
2½ tablespoons oil
40 g (1½ oz) softened butter
1 clove of garlic, crushed
2 tomatoes
1 tablespoon tomato purée
a bouquet garni
2 tablespoons cognac
5 tablespoons dry white wine
750 ml (1¼ pints) fish fumet (page 32)
5 tablespoons double cream
salt, freshly-ground pepper

Editor's note   Dealing with a live lobster at home is a problem – if possible ask your fishmonger to kill it for you and then hurry home and cook it. On a hot day take a cold insulated bag to carry it in. Remember that raw shellfish should be kept for a minimum of time as it deteriorates very rapidly. If you *are* stuck with doing the job yourself, however, the following method is probably the kindest. Cover the head with a cloth. Take a cleaver or heavy knife and, holding it parallel with the tail, bang it down sharply where the shell of the head meets the body. This will kill the creature instantly.
This soup can be made without the elvers if you cannot obtain them.

Preparation

1 Despatch the lobsters (see note, page 58) and cut them up as follows. Detach the tails and claws, split the body lengthwise down the middle, remove the stomach (a transparent pouch in the head) and put the coral, which is green in a raw lobster, in a bowl. Crack the claws and season everything with salt and pepper.

2 Cut the onion, the shallot and the carrot into mirepoix dice. Dip the tomatoes into boiling water for a few seconds, cut them in half, press the halves in the palm of your hand to squeeze out the pips and excess juice, and cut the pulp into dice.

3 Cook the elvers by throwing them into boiling water. When it comes back to the boil, skim the surface, allow to boil for 10 seconds and drain immediately in a colander.

Cooking

4 In a large saucepan heat the oil and 20 g ($\frac{3}{4}$ oz) butter. When they are very hot, throw in the pieces of lobster and turn them with a wooden spatula until they have become a beautiful red colour.

5 Add the vegetable mirepoix, cover the pan and simmer over a low heat for 5 minutes. Then add the crushed garlic, the fresh tomatoes and the tomato purée, and the bouquet garni. Deglaze the pan with the cognac, let it reduce and then add the white wine and the fish fumet. Cover the pan and simmer gently for 12 minutes.

6 Take out the pieces of lobster. Crush the heads of the lobsters in a liquidiser or food processor, return them to the pan and cook for a further 10 minutes. Meanwhile, extract the meat from the tails and claws, cut them into small dice and keep on one side.

7 Work the coral to a paste with 20 g ($\frac{3}{4}$ oz) of softened butter and mix it into the soup. Add the cream, bring to the boil and taste for seasoning – the flavour should be fairly intense. Strain through a fine conical strainer.

Serving

8 Place the diced lobster flesh and the elvers in the bottom of a soup tureen, pour the hot soup over the top and serve straight away.

Mussel Soup with Thyme Leaves

Soupe de moules à la feuille de thym

For four people
Preparation time: 35 minutes
Cooking time: 40 minutes

Ingredients

1 kg (2¼ lb) mussels
1 onion
a clove of garlic
the white part of a leek
1 carrot
3 tomatoes
5 tablespoons dry white wine
5 tablespoons double cream
3 tablespoons olive oil
500 ml (scant pint) fish fumet (page 32)
a bouquet garni
a pinch of saffron
a sprig of fresh thyme
salt, freshly-ground pepper

Preparation

1   Choose good mussels, alive and heavy with sea water, clean them and remove the beard, and wash them rapidly without leaving them to soak in the water.

2   Put them in a large saucepan, big enough to take twice their volume, pour in the white wine and cover with a well-fitting lid. Cook for about 4 minutes, shaking the pan from time to time. Once the mussels have opened, allow them to cool slightly and then remove them from their shells and put them into a bowl. Cover them with some of their cooking liquid strained through a conical strainer and strain the rest into a separate bowl.

3   Chop the onion, garlic and leek and cut the carrot into mirepoix dice. Plunge the tomatoes into boiling water for a few seconds, skin them, cut them in half and squeeze the halves in the palm of your hand to press out the pips and excess juice. Chop them coarsely.

4   Make up the bouquet garni. Rub the sprig of thyme between your fingers to detach the leaves from the stalks and keep them on one side.

Cooking

5   Heat the olive oil in a large saucepan and soften the onion, leek and carrot for 10 to 15 minutes without allowing them to brown. Add the garlic, the chopped tomatoes and the bouquet garni. Pour on the strained cooking liquid from the mussels and the fish fumet, bring to the boil and skim. Add the saffron and the salt, cover the pan and cook gently for 40 minutes.

6   Add the cream and bring to the boil, uncovered. Taste for seasoning, adding salt and pepper.

Serving

7   Put the mussels into the bottom of a heated soup tureen with 2 pinches of the thyme leaves and pour on the hot soup.

Salads

Salad of Young Spinach Leaves

Salade d'épinards nouveaux

For four people
Preparation time: 15 minutes

Ingredients 240 g (8½ oz) fresh young spinach leaves
2 hardboiled eggs
3 tablespoons lemon juice
140 ml (scant ¼ pint) olive oil
120 g (5 oz) smoked streaky bacon
2 tablespoons white wine vinegar
1 teaspoon pale Dijon mustard
salt, freshly-ground pepper

1 Choose tender young spinach, freshly picked, and remove the stalks. Wash in cold water, drain and pat dry with a cloth.

2 Pound the egg yolks and put them into a deep bowl, together with the mustard, the lemon juice and salt and pepper. Gradually incorporate the oil, a few drops at a time, whisking vigorously.

3 Chop the egg whites coarsely.

4 Cut the bacon into very fine strips or lardons and brown them in a frying-pan. When they are nicely crisp, pour off the excess fat.

5 To serve, put the spinach leaves in a salad bowl, pour on the egg-yolk dressing and toss the leaves with salad servers to mix the salad (the French word is 'fatiguer'). Sprinkle with the chopped egg whites and the hot lardons. Deglaze the frying-pan with the vinegar and sprinkle it onto the salad. At the table toss the salad again to mix everything together thoroughly.

Duck with Blackcurrants – *Canette aux baies de cassis* (page 150)

Pigeons with Garlic – *Pigeons aux gousses d'ail en chemise* (page 160)

Salad of Freshwater Crayfish Tails

Salade de queues d'écrevisses

For four people
Preparation time: 45 minutes
Cooking time: 8 minutes

Ingredients	80 freshwater crayfish **or** Dublin Bay prawns weighing about 3·5 kg (7 lb 14 oz) 20 leaves of curly endive 4 g (1 teaspoon) lobster eggs **or** paprika Cold Sauce for Shellfish Salads (page 40)

1 Prepare the shellfish according to the method given under the recipe on page 76, keeping four whole ones to decorate the salads.

2 Wash the endive and dry in a cloth.

3 Mix the shelled tails and the shellfish sauce together in a bowl. Arrange the endive in four little individual bowls with the leaves curling over the sides, fill with the shellfish mixture and place one of the whole crayfish or Dublin Bay prawns on the side of each bowl. Sprinkle the blanched lobster eggs, or the paprika, over the top of each salad.

* You can use the heads and shells of the shellfish to make a little bisque.

Salad of Hen Pheasants

Salade de faisanes

For four people
Preparation time: 45 minutes
Cooking time: 25 minutes

Ingredients
2 young hen pheasants weighing not more than
1 kg (2¼ lb) each in their feathers
20 g (¾ oz) butter
6 tablespoons walnut oil
3 tablespoons wine vinegar
2 heads of curly endive
2 tomatoes
16 walnuts
a slice off the crust of pain de campagne – a
slightly sour country bread – use light rye bread
as a substitute
3 cloves of garlic, unpeeled
a sprig of thyme
1 teaspoon Dijon mustard
salt, freshly-ground pepper

Preparing and cooking the pheasants

1 Choose 2 young hen pheasants which are not too damaged by shot and not 'high'. Pluck the birds, clean, singe and truss them or ask your gamemonger to do it for you.

2 Take an enamelled cast-iron pan large enough to hold the two birds side by side. Melt the butter in the pan and sauté the pheasants until they are a nice golden colour all over. Add two of the cloves of garlic, unpeeled, and the sprig of thyme, cover the pan and cook over a low heat for 25 minutes (see editor's note). Add a little water from time to time to give a good, deep brown 'jus' – not more than half a glass in all.

3 At the end of the cooking time, take out the birds and allow the fat to rise to the surface of the liquid so that it can be skimmed off. Add a little more liquid if necessary, reduce the 'jus' until there are 4 good tablespoons left and strain. Keep it warm.

Preparing the salad

4 While the pheasants are cooking, assemble the other ingredients. For the vinaigrette sauce, put the mustard, salt, pepper and vinegar into a salad bowl in that order and gradually add the walnut oil, whisking all the time.

5 Pick over the endive and detach the leaves, wash them thoroughly, dry them well and wrap loosely in a cloth. Plunge the tomatoes into boiling water for a few moments, skin them, cut them in half and squeeze out the pips and excess moisture in the palm of your hand. Then cut each half into six pieces, put them into a bowl and moisten lightly with 2 tablespoons of the vinaigrette. Shell the walnuts and reserve the kernels.

6 To make 'chapons', rub the slice of crust all over with the remaining clove of garlic, peeled. Cut into slices the thickness of a coin, to obtain five little oblong strips, and moisten them with a few drops of walnut oil.

Finishing and serving the salad

7 Remove the trussing strings from the pheasants and carve off the breasts, removing the skin. The wings and legs can be used to make a salmis. Cut the breasts into 5 cm (2 in) strips, or 'aiguillettes', arrange them on a serving dish and sprinkle with a little of the warm glaze.

8 Dress the endive with the vinaigrette sauce and arrange on four large plates. Arrange the 'aiguillettes' of pheasant on top and decorate with the pieces of tomato, the halved walnuts and the 'chapons'. Sprinkle the rest of the warm pheasant glaze over the salad at the last minute and serve immediately.

Editor's note The original cooking time of 25 minutes leaves the pheasants too underdone for most people's taste, so allow up to 45 minutes according to how well done you like your pheasants.

Salad of Foie Gras and Spinach

Salade nouvelle

For four people
Preparation time: 25 minutes
Cooking time: 2 minutes

Ingredients   280 g (9¾ oz) raw duck foie gras
240 g (8½ oz) fresh young spinach leaves
2 hardboiled eggs
juice of half a lemon
1 tablespoon white wine vinegar
2 tablespoons arachide oil
150 ml (¼ pint) virgin olive oil
1 teaspoon pale Dijon mustard
salt, freshly-ground pepper

A day in advance

1 Starting the day before you want to serve the salad, in order to give the foie gras time to become firm, prepare the livers by carefully removing nerves and connective tissues from between the two lobes. Plunge the foie gras into a saucepan of boiling salted water, bring back to the boil for one minute and leave to cool in the liquid. Leave it overnight in a cool place.

Preparation

2 Choose young, tender spinach and remove the stalks and ribs. Wash in plenty of water, drain well and pat it dry in a cloth.

3 To make the dressing, pound the egg yolks and mix in a salad bowl with the mustard, lemon juice and salt and pepper. Incorporate the olive oil little by little, whisking vigorously to emulsify the sauce.

4 Take the foie gras out of its cooking liquid and slice finely across its width into little escalopes weighing about 15 g ($\frac{1}{2}$ oz) each. Lay them side by side on a chopping board and season with salt and freshly-ground pepper.

Finishing and serving

5 Heat the oven to 220°C/425°F/Mark 7. Put the spinach into a salad bowl and toss with the dressing. Arrange on four heated plates.

6 Heat two large frying-pans, put a tablespoon of arachide oil into each one and when a haze rises from the pans brown the slices of foie gras for one minute on each side. Remove them and arrange the slices in a star on top of each plate of spinach.

7 Pour the fat out of the two frying-pans and deglaze them with the wine vinegar. Meanwhile put the plates of salad into the oven to keep hot, removing them after a few seconds. Using the back of a spoon dipped in the deglazing liquid, moisten the surface of each slice of foie gras, and serve at once.

Salad Riche

Salade riche

For four people
Preparation time: 30 minutes

Ingredients   120 g (5 oz) cooked foie gras (the potted kind that
     can be bought at very good food shops)
    24 freshwater crayfish **or** Dublin Bay prawns
    40 g (1½ oz) black truffles, cooked or tinned
    a small lettuce
    a small head of batavian endive
    a small curly endive
    4 leaves of red chicory (radicchio trevisano)
    2 hardboiled eggs
    a few lobster eggs **or** a tomato
    5 tablespoons walnut oil
    2½ tablespoons wine vinegar
    juice of ¼ lemon
    1 teaspoon of pale Dijon mustard
    1 litre (1¾ pints) court-bouillon for shellfish
    (page 33)
    salt, freshly-ground pepper

Preparation

1 Pick over and trim the various salad leaves, wash them thoroughly and dry in a cloth. Poach the shellfish for 2 minutes in the court-bouillon and shell the tails (see page 77).

2 Slice the truffles finely and season lightly with salt and pepper, the lemon juice and a few drops of walnut oil. If you are using the lobster eggs, put them in a sieve and blanch them in boiling water for a few seconds, refresh them under cold running water and drain. Otherwise, skin and deseed the tomato and cut it into small dice. Shell the eggs and cut the whites into fine rounds, keeping the yolks for another purpose.

3 Make the vinaigrette sauce. Put the mustard, wine vinegar, salt and pepper in a salad bowl and emulsify the sauce with a whisk, gradually incorporating the remaining walnut oil.

Serving

4 Moisten the shellfish with a tablespoon of the vinaigrette. Toss the different salad leaves together and dress with the sauce; divide them between four plates, putting one leaf of red chicory on each plate. Arrange the foie gras on top, cut in fine slices the thickness of a coin, break the slices of truffle into three or four pieces and alternate them with the rings of egg white to create a mosaic. Sprinkle the lobster eggs over the top, or failing that, use the diced tomato to add a touch of red.

* When fresh truffles are in season, they can be cooked in the following way:

> 140 g fresh truffles
> 1 tablespoon cognac
> 2 tablespoons dry white wine
> 200 ml ($\frac{1}{3}$ pint) water
> salt, freshly-ground pepper

Combine the cognac, wine, water and seasoning in a saucepan with a close-fitting lid. Brush the dirt carefully away from all the crevices in the truffles and peel them very, very thinly. (Put the peelings in a jar, cover them with cognac and use them to flavour sauces, etc.) Cook the truffles, hermetically sealed, over a gentle heat for 20 minutes and allow them to cool in their liquid. They can now be used in the same way as preserved or tinned truffles.

Light First Courses

Bouillon of Winter Snails

Bouillon d'escargots dormeurs

For four people
Preparation time: 1 hour
Cooking time: 40 minutes

Ingredients   40 snails
100 g (3½ oz) butter
a carrot
the white part of a leek
an onion
a stick of celery
5 tablespoons dry white wine
750 ml (1¼ pints) poultry stock (page 27)
a bouquet garni
basil (when available) **or** chervil
sea salt, freshly-ground pepper

Preparation

1   For this recipe you will only succeed if you can find snails which have retired into their shells to hibernate through the winter. Remove the hard 'front door' (operculum) with the point of a knife, wash the snails in plenty of water, disgorge for 2 hours with a handful of dry sea salt, then rinse. Put them in a saucepan of water and bring them to the boil, drain immediately. Pull out the flesh with a trussing needle or a fine knitting needle and remove the black part, known as the intestine, at the tail end of the snail. Put the snails in a saucepan, and keep them on one side.

2   Cut the carrot, leek, onion and celery into mirepoix dice and make up the bouquet garni.

Cooking

3   Heat 10 g ($\frac{1}{3}$ oz) butter in a fairly large saucepan and cook the vegetables gently for 4 or 5 minutes, stirring with a wooden spoon. Deglaze the pan with the white wine, reduce it by half and then add the stock. Bring to the boil and add the snails and the bouquet garni and a little salt. Simmer gently for 20 minutes.

4   Remove the pan from the heat and remove the snails to a small saucepan. Over a brisk heat add the butter to the broth in small pieces, whisking vigorously. When it has emulsified to a smooth liquid, pour it over the snails.

Serving

5   Divide the snails between four soup bowls, putting ten snails in each, pour over the broth, scatter coarsely chopped basil or chervil over the top and sprinkle two crystals of sea salt on any snails that have risen to the top.

Editor's note   You can substitute tinned snails for fresh snails to make this soup, but the taste will not be exactly the same.

Cassolette of Freshwater Crayfish with White Wine and Herbs

Cassolette de queues d'écrevisses

For four people
Preparation time: 1 hour
Cooking time: 10 minutes

Ingredients

80 live freshwater crayfish weighing about 3·5 kg (7 lb 14 oz)

150 ml ($\frac{1}{4}$ pint) dry white wine, preferably Sancerre

2 litres ($3\frac{1}{2}$ pints) court-bouillon (page 33)

140 g (5 oz) butter

juice of $\frac{1}{4}$ lemon

4 leaves of fresh tarragon, chopped

a sprig of flat-leaved or 'continental' parsley

salt, freshly-ground pepper

Editor's note   You can use raw Dublin Bay prawns to make this dish if you cannot obtain freshwater crayfish.

To cleanse live crayfish, put them into a bucket of water in which you have dissolved a couple of handfuls of dried milk powder and leave them in a cool place overnight. This cleans out the intestine.

Preparation

1 It is absolutely essential that the freshwater crayfish are live, there can be no exception to this rule. If they have not been cleansed (see note) you must clean them by removing the intestinal thread. Locate the middle ring of the body shell and the hole beneath it, take by the orifice and pull gently, giving a quarter turn and carefully drawing out the whole gut. It is a good idea to clean and cook the crayfish 20 at a time (in other words, four separate operations to deal with the 80) to prevent them starting to disintegrate while you perform this fairly lengthy operation – they will start to deteriorate from the moment the gut has been removed.

2 To cook the shellfish, bring the court-bouillon to the boil in a deep pan, throw them in, cover the pan and cook for 3 minutes. Take off the heat, let them cool slightly and shell the tails, keeping the tail meat on one side.

3 Remove the vegetables from the court-bouillon with a skimmer, discard the garlic and the bouquet garni and transfer the vegetables to a shallow pan. Add the white wine and boil it over a fierce heat until it has reduced to half its original volume. Then add the butter in small pieces and boil rapidly. Remove from the heat as soon as the sauce is the consistency of melted butter.

4 Add the shellfish tails, the lemon juice and the tarragon and taste for seasoning. Simmer very gently for 2 minutes, taking great care not to let it boil, so that the shellfish are very hot but still tender.

5 Divide the crayfish tails and their sauce between four small deep dishes, or 'cassolettes', arranging the carrots and onions in the form of rosettes on top, and sprinkle with one or two sprigs of flat parsley leaves.

Crépazes

For four people
Preparation time: 45 minutes
Cooking time: 20 minutes

Ingredients

70 g (2½ oz) lean cooked ham, sliced very thinly
70 g (2½ oz) lean raw ham, sliced very thinly
200 ml (⅓ pint) double cream
20 g (¾ oz) Gruyère cheese
salt, pepper

for the pancakes:
50 g (1¾ oz) plain flour
1 egg
6 tablespoons milk
15 g (½ oz) butter
arachide oil
salt, freshly-ground pepper

Preparation

1   To make the pancakes, whisk the flour, egg and salt together in a large bowl and gradually incorporate the milk a little at a time. Strain through a fine conical strainer. Melt the butter in a small sauté pan, add the mixture and whisk it in lightly.

2   Cut the cheese into thin strips. Bring the cream to the boil in a small saucepan, remove from the heat and season with salt and pepper.

3   Make 8 to 10 small pancakes, using a small frying-pan, or perhaps two pans, 12 cm (5 in) across, and frying them in a little arachide oil.

4   Cut the slices of ham into pieces 12 cm (5 in) across.

5   Preheat the oven to 200°C/400°F/Mark 6. In a buttered soufflé dish just large enough to take the pancakes, pile up the ingredients in layers. Start with a pancake, followed by a slice of ham, a tablespoon of cream, a pancake, a slice of raw ham, a tablespoon of cream, and so on until all are used up. Cook in the oven for about 15 minutes, until bubbling and hot all the way through.

6   Turn the whole construction onto a round heatproof dish, sprinkle with the strips of cheese and brown under the grill.

Serving

7   Cut into quarters, using a bread knife, and serve immediately.

Frogs' Legs in Champagne

Grenouilles au blanc de blancs

For four people
Preparation time: 20 minutes
Cooking time: 12 minutes

Ingredients

24 pairs of prepared frogs' legs
a little flour for dusting the frogs' legs
300 ml ($\frac{1}{2}$ pint) double cream
60 g (2 oz) butter
150 ml ($\frac{1}{4}$ pint) dry still champagne, preferably
  blanc de blancs
juice of $\frac{1}{4}$ lemon
2 shallots, finely chopped
a clove of garlic, finely chopped
parsley, finely chopped
salt, freshly-ground pepper

1   Remove the frogs from the skewers and with a pair of scissors cut away the front part of the body and the feet. Season them with salt and pepper, roll them in flour and place in a colander.

2   Heat the butter to a hazelnut-brown colour in a large frying-pan, and arrange the frogs breast downwards in the pan without overlapping. As soon as they are golden, turn them over one at a time with a fork and brown the other side. All the butter should have been absorbed. Keep the frogs' legs hot in a fireproof serving dish.

3   Soften the shallots in the same pan for 30 seconds and then deglaze with the champagne. Let it reduce to three quarters of its volume and then add the cream. Bring it to the boil, whisking all the time, and let it boil for 1 or 2 minutes to produce a light smooth sauce.

4   Place the serving dish over the heat and coat the frogs with the sauce. Add the finely chopped garlic and parsley and taste for seasoning, adding salt and pepper if necessary. Simmer gently for a minute, then add the lemon juice and serve piping hot.

* The best season for frogs is springtime. They can now be bought ready-prepared, sometimes in pairs on skewers, and we don't need to worry about the difficult and unpleasant job of dissecting them.

Editor's note   Frogs, although not commonly eaten outside France, can now be obtained frozen from high-class grocers and delicatessens. They may be sold as single legs, in which case you will need 48 legs instead of 24 pairs.

Sweetbreads in Flaky Pastry

Coffrets de ris de veau

For four people
Preparation time: 1 hour
Cooking time: 40 minutes

Ingredients

600 g (1 lb 5 oz) veal sweetbreads
250 g (8¾ oz) leaf spinach
an onion
a carrot
a bouquet garni
1 large clove of garlic, peeled
2 tablespoons dry white wine
1 litre (1¾ pints) poultry stock (page 27)
1 tablespoon plain flour
55 g (2 oz) butter
250 ml (scant half pint) double cream
200 g (7 oz) homemade flaky pastry (page 36)
   or frozen flaky pastry
1 egg
juice of ¼ lemon
salt, freshly-ground pepper

Preparing and cooking the sweetbreads

1 Choose good veal sweetbreads, making sure that they are very
white and very fresh and soak them for 5 to 6 hours in cold water,
to disgorge.

2 Put the sweetbreads in a fairly generous saucepan with plenty
of cold water and bring slowly to the boil so that the sweetbreads
heat through gradually and become firm. When the water comes to
the boil remove it from the heat and leave them in the hot liquid
for 5 minutes, then refresh under cold running water and drain.
Separate the two parts of the sweetbreads – the 'gorge' or throat,
which is elongated, and the 'noix', which is round. Remove the outer
membranes and extract the nerves and veins.

3 Cook the spinach in the classic way (see page 220). Cut the carrot and onion into thin rounds.

4 Take a wide saucepan with a heavy base, it should be large enough to hold the sweetbreads without crowding. Put in the carrot and onion and the bouquet garni, place the sweetbreads on top and let them sweat for 10 minutes. Add the white wine and boil until evaporated. Then add the stock, cover the pan and simmer for 40 minutes. At the end of the cooking time, remove the sweetbreads and let them cool.

5 While the sweetbreads are cooling make a roux in a saucepan with half the butter and the flour and moisten with the cooking liquid. Cook for 20 minutes, add the cream, bring back to the boil for 2 minutes and remove from the heat.

The flaky pastry

6 Preheat the oven to 180°C/350°F/Mark 4. The pastry should be at the stage where it has had 5 folds and has just rested for a few minutes in a cool place. Roll it out thinly and evenly just under 1 cm ($\frac{1}{4}$ in) thick, lightly rolling the pin in all directions. With a knife cut out 4 rectangles 6 cm by 8 cm ($1\frac{1}{4}$ in by 3 in), making clean cuts, and arrange on a baking sheet, lightly moistened with water. Beat the egg and use it to glaze the top of the pastry with a brush. Cook for 20 minutes in the oven, then turn it off and let the pastry rest for 20 minutes in a covered dish.

Finishing and serving

7 Skin the sweetbreads, using your thumb and index finger, and separate them into their natural divisions. Put them into a saucepan, pour in the sauce, taste for seasoning and add the lemon juice.

8 Warm the spinach in the remaining butter heated to a clear hazelnut brown (beurre noisette), stirring with a fork with the clove of garlic spiked onto the prongs.

9 Put the pastry cases on four serving plates and lift off the top layer or lid of pastry. Hollow out the middles of the pastries and fill with the spinach, then divide the sweetbread mixture equally between the four. Replace the pastry lids and serve at once.

Snails with Herb Butter

Escargots de Bourgogne poêlés

For four people
Preparation time: 1 hour
Cooking time: 4 hours

Ingredients | *for cooking the snails:*

for cooking the snails:
40 snails
half a carrot, peeled
half an onion
clove of garlic, unpeeled
5 tablespoons dry white wine
a small bouquet garni
10 peppercorns, coarsely crushed
2 cloves
8 g ($\frac{1}{4}$ oz) sea salt

for the snail butter:
100 g ($3\frac{1}{2}$ oz) softened butter
a shallot
10 g ($\frac{1}{3}$ oz) parsley, chopped
clove of garlic, crushed
salt, freshly-ground pepper

Editor's note In some of the better French restaurants a special saucespoon, looking something like a miniature silver shovel, is provided to eat dishes served with a lot of delicate sauce. An ordinary spoon would do quite as well.

Preparation

1 If the snails are hibernating (November to March), use the same method of preparation as for the broth (page 75); if they are active (March to April), leave them in salt for 12 hours instead of the usual 2.

2 Shred the shallot finely and mix with the softened butter, the parsley and the crushed garlic to obtain a thick cream. Season with salt and pepper and work the cream through a sieve.

Cooking

3 Put the shelled snails into a large saucepan and add the carrot, the onion stuck with the cloves, the bouquet garni, the unpeeled clove of garlic, the white wine and the pepper. Cover with the same volume of water, plus one third more, add the sea salt, bring to the boil and skim away the scum which rises to the surface. Lower the heat until the liquid just trembles and simmer for $3\frac{1}{2}$ hours. When the snails are cooked, put them into an earthenware dish, together with their cooking liquid.

Finishing and serving

4 Five minutes before serving, drain the snails, and put them into a shallow pan; moisten them with 4 tablespoons of the cooking juice and simmer until the liquid has reduced to a generous tablespoon. Then add the butter in small bits and bring to the boil over a fierce heat, stirring with a wooden spoon. As it melts, the butter emulsifies with the liquid to make a thick sauce.

5 Divide the snails between four small, deep ovenproof dishes (cassolettes) and serve very hot. Eat them with a flat saucespoon.

Sautéed Duck Foie Gras with Celeriac

Foie gras de canard sauté aux céleris boules

For four people
Preparation time: 30 minutes
Cooking time: 2 minutes

Ingredients   500 g (1 lb 2 oz) raw duck foie gras
200 g (7 oz) celeriac
30 g (1 oz) truffles
2½ tablespoons truffle juice, from the tin or the
   cooking liquid
250 ml (scant half pint) demi-glace (page 29)
2½ tablespoons port
40 g (1½ oz) butter
salt, freshly-ground pepper

Preparation and cooking

1 Prepare the foie gras a day in advance. First remove the nerves and sinews from between the lobes of the liver. Plunge into boiling salted water for one minute, remove the pan from the heat, leave the livers in the liquid and keep in a cool place overnight.

2 Separate the two lobes of the livers and make sure that there are no greenish traces left by the gall-bladder. Dip a knife in hot water and cut the liver into slices 1·5 cm ($\frac{1}{2}$ in) thick. Place the slices in a dish, cover with silver foil and keep in a cool place.

3 Peel the celeriac, cut it into small fat sticks 3 cm (1 in) long and then, using a small sharp knife, 'turn' them like a woodcarver into the shape of cloves of garlic. Put them into a saucepan, cover them with cold water, bring them to the boil, then drain and refresh them under cold water. Now cook them in boiling salted water in the same saucepan. They should retain some 'bite'; they are done when they feel slightly soft to the touch. Refresh under cold running water and drain.

4 Cut the truffles into little dice. In a medium-sized saucepan, heat a walnut of butter and sauté the truffles for 2 minutes. Deglaze the pan with the port, let it evaporate and then add the truffle juice and the demi-glace. Simmer very gently for 10 minutes over a very low flame, skimming away any scum that rises to the surface. Meanwhile sauté the celeriac for a minute or two, with a walnut of butter, in a small frying-pan. At the last minute, thicken the truffle sauce with 25 g (1 oz) of butter, check the seasoning and add the celeriac.

Finishing and serving

5 Heat the rest of the butter over a fierce flame in a frying-pan large enough to hold all the slices of foie gras. Slide in the foie gras, season with salt and pepper and cook for one minute on each side.

6 Divide the slices between four plates, coat lightly with the boiling truffle sauce and arrange the celeriac prettily on top.

Oysters with Winkles

Huîtres chaudes 'aux bigorneaux'

For four people
Preparation time: 40 minutes
Cooking time: 20 minutes

Ingredients	12 'Belon' oysters
	12 'Portuguese' oysters
	12 dozen winkles
	2 carrots, sliced
	an onion, sliced
	a stick of celery, sliced
	a sprig of thyme
	220 g (7¾ oz) butter
	2½ tablespoons distilled vinegar
	juice of half a lemon
	salt, freshly-ground pepper

(see colour illustration opposite page 80)

Preparation and cooking

1 First open the 'Belon' oysters over a small saucepan, catching all the liquid they contain. Detach the oysters and put them into the pan with their liquid, taking care to remove the different foreign bodies (pieces of shell, etc.). Repeat the process with the 'Portuguese' oysters using a separate saucepan, and place the hollow shells of both varieties in two ovenproof dishes.

2 Make a court-bouillon in a saucepan with the carrot, onion, celery and thyme, a handful of sea salt, the vinegar and 1 litre (1¾ pints) water. Bring it to the boil and cook for 15 minutes. Meanwhile, wash the winkles and throw them into the boiling court-bouillon, bring it back to the boil, skim away the scum that rises to the surface and cook the winkles for 3 minutes. Take the pan off the heat and let the winkles cool a little in their liquid until you can pick them up in your fingers. Extract the creatures from their shells with a large pin, removing the intestine or cloaca, the black part at the end, and put them on one side in a bowl.

3 Strain 5 tablespoons of the winkle cooking liquid into a small saucepan and place over a fierce heat. Add the butter in little pieces working it up with a whisk until you have a smooth sauce. Taste for seasoning, being very generous with pepper, and add the lemon juice.

4 Heat the oysters in their respective saucepans, bringing them to a maximum temperature of 60° C/120° F. This should take no longer than 2 minutes over a medium heat.

Finishing and serving

5 Heat the empty oyster shells in the oven and put the appropriate variety of oyster into each one. Arrange six winkles on each oyster and cover lightly with the sauce. Place the oysters under a hot grill for 20 seconds and serve at once, putting three oysters of each type on each plate.

Flan of Loire Sander (Pike-perch)

Quiche au sandre de Loire

For four people
Preparation time: 45 minutes
Cooking time: 30 minutes

Ingredients   1 sander or pike-perch weighing 700 g (1 lb 9 oz)
750 ml (1¼ pints) court-bouillon (page 33)
300 g (10½ oz) yeast pastry (page 34)
2 tablespoons double cream
4 eggs
salt, freshly-ground pepper
butter sauce (page 217)

Editor's note   Pike-perch or sander, which is a delicate finned fresh-water fish with an excellent flavour and texture, is sometimes available from good fishmongers. (It is apparently becoming quite common in East Anglia where it has naturalised in the dykes and is rapidly taking over from the local inhabitants.)

Preparation and cooking

1 Clean, gut and fillet the fish and place, skin side down, in a wide shallow pan. Cover with the court-bouillon, salt if necessary and simmer over a gentle heat for 3 minutes. Take out the fillets, let them cool and drain, then lift off the skin and put them on a serving dish.

2 Preheat the oven to 180° C/350° F/Mark 4. Lightly flour the working surface and roll out the pastry into a circle about 26 cm (10 in) in diameter. Put a 20 cm (8 in) flan ring on a baking sheet and line it carefully with pastry, making certain that it is over the middle of the flan ring before you lower it into place. Press the pastry into the sides, cut off surplus pastry which hangs over the edge by rolling the pin over the flan ring and pinch up the edges. Prick the base with a fork, line the flan case with greaseproof paper, fill it with dried beans, and bake blind for 10 minutes.

3 Using a small whisk, mix the cream, eggs and salt and pepper in a bowl, then strain through a fine conical strainer into another bowl.

4 Remove the paper and beans from the flan, fill with the fish, put the baking sheet on the oven-rack ready to slide it straight into the oven, and pour on the filling. Bake for 15 minutes at 160° C/300° F/Mark 2, remove from the oven and let it rest for 5 minutes.

Serving

5 Slide the flan onto a flat round plate, lift off the ring and serve accompanied by a butter sauce (see the recipe for Roanne Ham with Ribbon Vegetables, page 217)

Little Truffle Turnovers

Ragoût de truffes en chaussons

For four people
Preparation time: 30 minutes
Cooking time: 20 minutes

Ingredients   250 g (8¾ oz) homemade flaky pastry (page 36) or
frozen flaky pastry
1 egg, beaten
200 g (7 oz) truffles, fresh or tinned
1 shallot, finely chopped
10 g (⅓ oz) cooked foie gras (from a jar or tin will
do)
20 g (¾ oz) butter
1 tablespoon cognac
5 tablespoons truffle juice
250 ml (scant half pint) double cream
salt, freshly-ground pepper

Preparation and cooking

1 Preheat the oven to 180° C/350° F/Mark 4. Place the flaky pastry, which should be rested and very firm, on a marble top or very cold working surface and roll out to about 6 mm ($\frac{1}{4}$ in) thick. With a pastry cutter or an upturned glass, cut into two circles 8 cm ($3\frac{1}{2}$ in) in diameter. Then cut each in half to give four turnovers and place them on a lightly dampened baking sheet.

2 Paint the top of the pastry with a pastry brush dipped in the beaten egg, making certain that the egg doesn't run down the sides, which would, as it cooked and hardened, prevent the pastry from rising evenly. Make your pattern on each turnover with the back of a knife, cutting lightly to a depth of about 1 mm. Cook in the oven for 15 minutes until the turnovers are well risen and then keep hot.

3 Cut the truffles into pieces 4 cm ($1\frac{1}{2}$ in) long, each weighing about 5 g ($\frac{1}{5}$ oz). Purée the foie gras by working it through a fine wire sieve.

4 Melt the butter in a shallow saucepan and soften the shallot without letting it brown. Add the truffles, season with salt and pepper, cover the pan and simmer gently for 2 minutes. Deglaze the pan with the cognac, add the truffle juice and bring it back to the boil. Then add the cream and let it simmer very gently until you have a light sauce. Add the foie gras, and shake the pan, to emulsify the sauce. Taste for seasoning.

Serving

5 Half open the turnovers with the point of a knife, place them on four heated plates and distribute the truffle mixture so that it runs over the edges a little. Serve at once.

Fillets of Raw Salmon and John Dory with Salt-cod Seasoning

Saumon et saint-pierre crus au sel de morue

For four people
Preparation time: 15 minutes

Ingredients

200 g (7 oz) fillets of fresh salmon
200 g (7 oz) fillets of John Dory
60 g (2 oz) very very dry salt cod
juice of a lemon
8 white peppercorns, coarsely crushed
(mignonette pepper)
32 coriander seeds
4 tarragon leaves
sprigs of flat parsley
160 ml ($\frac{1}{4}$ pint) virgin olive oil
4 slices pain de campagne (use homemade light brown bread as a substitute)

1 Chill four plates in the refrigerator. Cut the fish fillets into very fine strips with a fine, flexible knife making sure that there is no skin or slime on them. Arrange them prettily on the plates, alternating the colours of the two fish and giving them an undulating effect, like waves.

2 Take a small piece of very dry salt cod, rub it through a cheese grater and sift the powder through a fine sieve. Scatter this salt over the fish fillets.

3 Sprinkle the whole surface of the fish fillets with lemon juice. Divide the mignonette pepper and the coriander seeds between the plates and strew with the chopped tarragon. Slip the little leaves of parsley in between the two types of fish. Chill in the refrigerator for 15 minutes.

4 Pour the olive oil all over the fillets in a thin stream and serve immediately with large slices of grilled pain de campagne.

Editor's note Plain course salt can be substituted for salt-cod salt for those who do not like the flavour of salt cod.
Light rye, which sometimes makes a good substitute for pain de campagne, would be too strong flavoured for this interesting dish. Homemade bread made with about half 80% wheatmeal and half unbleached white flour would be a better alternative.

Truffle Soufflé

Soufflé aux truffes

For four people
Preparation time: 25 minutes
Cooking time: 10 minutes

Ingredients   80 g (2¾ oz) butter
40 g (1½ oz) flour
250 ml (scant half pint) milk
140 g (5 oz) preserved truffles
5 tablespoons truffle juice, from the tin
4 eggs
salt

Editor's note   If you want to use fresh truffles, the recipe for cooking them can be found on page 71.

Preparation and cooking

1   Melt 60 g (2 oz) butter in a small saucepan over a low heat. Add the flour and stir with a whisk for 3 minutes without allowing it to start browning. Gradually add the milk and the truffle juice to the roux, stirring vigorously all the time to prevent lumps. Season lightly with salt and continue to stir until it comes to the boil. Then leave the pan over a very low heat for 20 minutes, and let it cook very very gently, without letting it boil. You can slightly raise one edge of the saucepan by putting a skewer under one side, or use an asbestos mat. When the sauce is ready, strain it through a very fine conical strainer into a large saucepan, helping it through with the whisk.

2   Cut four nice slices of truffle on a mandoline and keep them on one side. Cut 100 g (3½ oz) of the truffles into small cubes and add them to the sauce.

3   Butter four ramekins or individual soufflé dishes with the rest of the butter – 20 g (¾ oz) – and line with the remaining truffles, finely chopped.

4   Preheat the oven to 200° C/400° F/Mark 6. Put the egg whites into a copper bowl, and add a pinch of fine salt. Whisk the whites to a snow until they are just firm enough to hold together in a mass, but no longer. As soon as they are ready, add the egg yolks to the warm sauce, stir them in thoroughly, add a quarter of the whites and mix again. This helps to soften the mixture and make it easier to incorporate the rest of the whites, which should be done by folding them lightly in with a spatula until you have a uniform mass. Heat a baking sheet in the oven.

5   Fill the four ramekins or soufflé dishes with the mixture so that they are four fifths full and place them on the heated baking sheet for 2 minutes to help them to rise. Then cook in the oven for about 10 minutes, checking to see when they are done.

Serving

6   Decorate each soufflé with a slice of truffle and serve at once.

Cantal Cheese Tart

Tarte à la Fourme du Cantal

For four people
Preparation time: 25 minutes
Cooking time: 20 minutes

Ingredients

150 g (5¼ oz) homemade flaky pastry (page 36) or frozen flaky pastry

3 ripe round medium tomatoes weighing 100 g (3½ oz) each

2 tablespoons virgin olive oil

180 g (6¼ oz) cheese, Fourme du Cantal **or** Cheddar

1 tablespoon tarragon mustard

salt, pepper

Preparation

1   Roll out the pastry into a round 26 cm (10 in) in diameter. Place a 20 cm (8 in) flan ring on a lightly moistened baking sheet and lower the pastry over the centre of the ring. Cut off the extra pastry round the edges with the rolling-pin. Press the pastry down into the corners of the ring so that it doesn't break when you take it out, and pinch up the edges. Lightly prick the base with the point of a knife and keep in a cool place.

2   Slice the tomatoes across into rounds 1 cm ($\frac{1}{2}$ in) thick and discard the top and bottom slices. Taking care not to break them, remove all the pips carefully from each slice. Arrange on a plate, season with salt and pepper and coat with the olive oil. Leave them to marinate for 15 minutes, turning them over two or three times.

3   Remove the rind and cut the cheese into slices 6 mm ($\frac{1}{4}$ in) thick.

Cooking and serving

4   Preheat the oven to 180° C/350° F/Mark 4. Spread the mustard over the base of the tart, cover with the cheese and arrange the tomato slices prettily on top. Sprinkle the tomato marinade over all. Bake for 20 minutes in the oven.

5   Let the flan rest for 15 minutes, to allow the filling to set a little, slide it onto a round plate, removing the ring, and cut into four. The flan is best eaten lukewarm, as it will be after resting for 15 minutes, although you can serve it hot straight from the oven.

Terrine of Vegetables 'Olympe'

Terrine de légumes 'Olympe'

For eight people
Preparation time: 2 hours
Cooking time: 30 minutes

Ingredients

150 g (5½ oz) small, thin French beans (haricots verts)
150 g (5½ oz) peas (preferably petits pois), fresh or frozen
6 medium globe artichokes
10 g (½ oz) butter
150 g (5½ oz) small new carrots
12 vineleaves **or,** failing these, 4 lemons
salt

for the farce:
450 g (1 lb) mild ham
1½ egg whites
juice of a lemon
9 tablespoons arachide oil
6 g (scant teaspoon) salt
a little freshly-ground pepper
Cold Tomato Sauce 'Jean Yanne' (page 44)

Preparing the vegetables

1   Cook the beans and the peas separately in plenty of boiling water, keeping them rather underdone. Refresh under cold water, and leave to cool. Cook the carrots whole in boiling water, drain, refresh and cool them.

2   Break off the artichoke stalks, remove the leaves and trim the bases. Plunge them at once into a bowl of water acidulated with lemon juice to prevent them from discolouring. Heat the butter in a fairly large saucepan, big enough to hold the artichoke bottoms side by side, and sweat them for 7 to 8 minutes. Pour on enough water to cover, cover the hearts with greaseproof paper, put on the

lid and leave to cook gently for 20 minutes. Leave them to cool and then remove the chokes, trim the hearts and cut them in half.

The farce

3 The farce must be made very quickly and with the container of the liquidiser or food processor well chilled in the refrigerator.

4 Carefully remove the sinews and gristle from the ham. Chop into small dice and chill in the refrigerator for at least 30 minutes.

5 Put the ham and the egg white into the chilled liquidiser or food processor and season with salt and pepper. Set the machine at its highest speed and gradually add the lemon juice and the arachide oil. This must all be done very quickly so that the farce does not have time to get warm.

Cooking

6 Preheat the oven to 150° C/300° F/Mark 2. Take a rectangular terrine, 22 cm (9 in) long, 12 cm (5 in) across and 6 cm (2½ in) high. Line the bottom and sides with the vineleaves or with the lemons, peeled with a sharp knife to remove both skin and pith and thinly sliced.

7 Assemble the cold vegetables and make up the terrine. Spread a fine layer of the farce in the bottom of the dish, cover with a row of carrots, and then arrange layers of the other vegetables – beans, artichokes and peas – putting a layer of farce in between and finishing with a layer of farce. Cover with a sheet of buttered greaseproof paper and cook in the oven, in a bain-marie, for 30 minutes. Then chill in the refrigerator for at least 8 hours.

Serving

8 Turn out the terrine. Take eight chilled plates and pour a ladleful of Cold Tomato Sauce 'Jean Yanne' (page 44) onto each. Arrange two slices of the terrine, 1·5 cm (½ in) thick, on top.

Editor's note This is a lovely summer dish, best if made with fresh vegetables. It is named after Madame Olympe, Pierre Troisgros' wife.

(see colour illustration opposite page 225)

Veal and Potato Pie with Chives

Tourte de pommes de terre

For four people
Preparation time: 40 minutes
Cooking time: 45 minutes

Ingredients 300 g (10½ oz) potatoes
150 g (5¼ oz) veal fillet
2 shallots
20 g (¾ oz) butter
10 chives
a sprig of chervil
250 g (8¾ oz) homemade flaky pastry (page 36) or
frozen flaky pastry
1 egg, beaten
5 tablespoons double cream
salt, freshly-ground pepper

Preparation and cooking

1   Peel and wash the potatoes and slice them on a mandoline into rounds 5 mm ($\frac{1}{4}$ in) thick; put the slices into a bowl. Remove the sinews and gristle from the veal and cut it into very thin strips. Chop the shallots finely and soften them in the butter in a small frying-pan for 2 minutes. Cut up the chives with scissors and take the chervil leaves off their stalks. Mix all these ingredients with the potatoes and season with salt and pepper.

2   Preheat the oven to 200° C/400° F/Mark 6. Roll out two circles of flaky pastry on your worktop, 18 cm (7 in) and 22 cm (9 in) in diameter. Moisten a baking sheet with water and place the smaller pastry circle on it. Cover with the potato and veal mixture, leaving a margin of 2 cm ($\frac{3}{4}$ in) round the edge. Moisten the edge and then cover with the second, larger pastry circle. Pinch the edges over each other so that the flan is hermetically sealed. Brush the surface with a pastry brush dipped in beaten egg. Make a deep circle 10 cm (4 in) in diameter on the top using the back of a knife and decorate it with a pattern you like. Bake in the oven for 30 minutes.

3   Heat the cream in a small saucepan. When the flan is done, take it out of the oven, lift its 'lid' (cutting round the circle that you made with the knife) and pour in the boiling cream, gently lifting the potato mixture so that it spreads evenly through the pie. Replace the lid and return the pie to the oven for another 15 minutes. Then take it out and let it rest for a quarter of an hour.

Serving

4   Slide the pie onto a round plate decorated with a lace paper mat and slice with a large knife.

* The pie can be served simply with melted butter or with a green salad dressed with walnut oil.

* This dish is adapted from an old Bourbonnaise recipe, known as 'pâté au tartouffe'.

Eggs

Scrambled Eggs with Fresh Sea-urchins

Oeufs brouillés aux oursins

For four people
Preparation time: 20 minutes
Cooking time: 10 minutes

Ingredients   1·5 kg (3 lb 6 oz) live sea-urchins
10 eggs
70 g ($2\frac{1}{2}$ oz) softened butter
salt, freshly-ground pepper

Preparation

1 If possible, choose sea-urchins of a good purple colour, at the peak of freshness and heavy with sea water. To open them, cut a round hole with a pair of scissors a quarter of the way down from the concave end where the mouth of the creature is located. With the back of a spoon, detach the yellow 'coral', which is fixed to the wall of the shell, and transfer it to a small saucepan. Choose 8 to 12 of the best shells, depending on their size, wash them and set them on one side.

2 Break the eggs into a large bowl, add salt and beat them lightly with a fork, adding 50 g (1¾ oz) butter in little pieces.

Cooking and serving

3 Butter a tinned copper pan with a heavy base and place over a very low flame. Pour in the beaten eggs and stir continuously in all directions with a wooden spoon to mix the liquid part evenly with the parts that are beginning to set. As soon as you notice a slight thickening, remove the pan to the side of the heat without stopping your careful stirring, and let the eggs finish cooking in their own heat and the heat of the pan. When they have become an even, creamy consistency, season them lightly with pepper.

4 At the same time, heat the saucepan containing the coral of sea-urchins very gently without boiling, take it off the heat and thicken with 10 g (⅓ oz) butter by shaking the pan.

5 Heat the reserved urchin shells and fill them with scrambled eggs, covering the top with coral.

Poached Eggs 'Bodin'

Oeufs pochés Bodin

For four people
Preparation time: 1 hour
Cooking time: 30 minutes

Ingredients 150 g (5¼ oz) haricots verts (French beans)
4 small tomatoes
a sprig of thyme
choux pastry for 4 puffs (page 38) or 4 large
   ready-made puffs
4 eggs
2½ tablespoons distilled wine vinegar, preferably
   aged
30 g (1 oz) butter
salt, freshly-ground pepper

Editor's note   Michel Bodin is a senior member of the kitchen staff
in the Troisgros restaurant and this recipe was named in his honour.

Preparation and cooking

1   Throw the beans into a saucepan of boiling salted water and bring back to the boil. Boil rapidly over a high heat for between 10 and 20 minutes, depending on the size of the beans, until just cooked. Refresh in a bowl of ice-cold water, drain them and purée through the fine blade of a mouli-légumes.

2   Preheat the oven to 180° C/350° F/Mark 4. Put the tomatoes into a small saucepan, crush them up with a wooden fork, add the thyme and salt and cook for about 20 minutes. Purée in a mouli-légumes and return to the pan. (If using a liquidiser, skin the tomatoes before cooking and strain the purée through a fine sieve.) Simmer the tomato purée until it has thickened to a light sauce.

3   Fill a forcing bag with the choux pastry and form four large puffs on a buttered baking sheet. Bake them for 20 minutes. If you are using ready-made puffs, heat them through in a slow oven.

4   Fill a wide shallow saucepan with water and add the vinegar but no salt. When the water is boiling nicely, break in the eggs quickly, one at a time. Shape the whites round the yolks with a wooden spatula and, as soon as the water has come back to the boil, take the pan off the heat and leave the eggs to poach for 2 minutes. Carefully remove the eggs with a skimmer and put them into a bowl of warm water to keep hot.

Finishing and serving

5   Heat the French bean purée in 15 g ($\frac{1}{2}$ oz) of butter heated to a hazelnut brown (beurre noisette). Then return to the boil, work in the remaining butter – 15 g ($\frac{1}{2}$ oz) – and season with salt and pepper. Plunge the eggs for a few minutes into a saucepan of hot but not boiling water.

6   Cut the tops off the puffs three quarters of the way up, reserving the lids. Fill each one with the French bean purée, put the well-drained eggs on top, coat with the tomato sauce and replace the lids. Serve at once, very hot.

Hardboiled Eggs 'Villemont'

Oeufs durs Villemont

For four people
Preparation time: 50 minutes
Cooking time: 20 minutes

Ingredients

300 g (10½ oz) new onions
half a red pepper
50 g (1¾ oz) Swiss chard leaves
10 g (⅓ oz) flour
75 g (2½ oz) butter
5 tablespoons milk
150 ml (¼ pint) double cream
8 eggs
nutmeg
salt, freshly-ground pepper

1   Peel and halve the onions and cut away 5 mm ($\frac{1}{4}$ in) from the root end of each half; this part may be bitter and in any case prevents the rings from separating properly. Then slice as finely and evenly as possible. Cut the pepper into thin strips. Wash the raw chard leaves and slice them coarsely.

2   Heat the butter in a shallow sauté pan and, as soon as it is melted, add the onions and strips of pepper. Brown for 5 minutes, stirring with a wooden spatula. Cover the pan and let them stew gently over a low heat for about 15 minutes. Add the chard leaves and let them soften for 5 minutes without browning. Sprinkle with the flour and stir for a few moments, then add the warmed milk a little at a time, stirring energetically to get rid of any lumps. Season with salt and pepper and a pinch of grated nutmeg and let it cook very gently for 20 minutes. Add the cream and bring back to the boil. Taste for seasoning.

3   While the sauce is cooking, make sure that the eggs are not flawed. To do this, tap them together lightly close to your ear and if they make a noise like cracked china, keep the cracked egg for something else. Put the sound eggs carefully into a colander and plunge it into a large saucepan of boiling salted water for 9 minutes. Leave them under the cold tap until they are cool enough to handle, then shell them and keep in a saucepan of hot, slightly-salted water.

4   Halve the eggs and arrange in a fireproof china dish (eggs will leave marks on silver). Cover with the sauce, let them cook very gently over a low heat for a minute or two and serve.

* Towards the end of the season when they are not so new, it is a good idea to blanch the sliced onions for 5 minutes in boiling water.

Watercress Omelette

Omelette à la chiffonnade de cresson

For four people
Preparation time: 20 minutes
Cooking time: 20 minutes

Ingredients 500 g (18 oz) watercress or 4 bunches
80 g (2¾ oz) softened butter
1 shallot, finely chopped
1 clove of garlic, peeled
8 eggs
salt, freshly-ground pepper

1 Wash the watercress and remove the stalks. Reserve 24 leaves for decoration. Melt 40 g (1½ oz) butter in a medium-sized sauté pan, and soften the chopped shallot. Add the watercress and season. Cover the pan and stew gently over a low heat for 20 minutes. When the watercress has melted down spread it out on a board and cut it into shreds with a knife. In a small saucepan, heat 20 g (¾ oz) butter to a hazelnut brown (beurre noisette), add the watercress and stir with a fork with the clove of garlic impaled on the prongs. Taste for seasoning. Put the reserved watercress leaves into a sieve and plunge them into a pan of boiling water for a second.

2 Break the eggs into a mixing bowl, season with salt and pepper and beat carefully with 10 g (⅓ oz) butter in little pieces. Heat all but a small nut of the remaining butter in a hot frying-pan and, when it is foaming, pour in the beaten eggs, stir quickly with a wooden fork and draw into the centre the bits of egg which are already set. Shake the pan so that the mass takes shape while still remaining creamy. When it has almost set but is still juicy, tip the omelette to one side of the pan.

3 Fill the inside of the omelette with the hot watercress, and roll it onto a serving plate. Rub the surface with a nut of butter to make it shine and decorate with the reserved blanched watercress leaves and eat immediately.

Boiled Eggs with Small Shrimps

Oeufs coque aux crevettes grises

For four people
Preparation time: 30 minutes
Cooking time: 3 minutes

Ingredients 8 very fresh eggs
250 g (8¾ oz) cooked small brown shrimps
5 g (1 teaspoon) butter
a quarter of a shallot, chopped
a long French loaf

1   Shell the shrimps and cut into three or four pieces the size of a grain of rice. Chop the shallot and sweat in the butter in a small saucepan, add the shrimps and let them just heat through without cooking.

2   Make sure that the eggs are not cracked (see recipe on page 111) and are at room temperature. Cook them in the classic way, plunging them into boiling water for 3 minutes.

3   Slice the tops off the eggs, remove the white from the lid with a teaspoon and fill the hollow tops with shrimps. Place the eggs in egg cups and turn the lids upside down on top, moving quickly so that the shrimps don't fall out. Cut narrow strips, 5 cm (2 in) in length, out of a long French loaf and use these 'soldiers' to eat with the eggs.

Fried Poached Eggs with Purée Stéphanoise

Oeufs pochés et frits à la purée Stéphanoise

For four people
Preparation time: 25 minutes
Cooking time: 1 hour 30 minutes

Ingredients Green Vegetable Purée (page 240)
7 eggs
2½ tablespoons white vinegar
20 g (¾ oz) butter
20 g (¾ oz) flour
300 ml (½ pint) poultry stock (page 27)
4 tablespoons cream
2 tablespoons arachide oil
fresh breadcrumbs
oil for frying
salt, pepper

1 Pour 1 litre (1¾ pints) water into a shallow pan – it should be about three quarters full. Add the vinegar, but no salt, and bring it to the boil. One by one, break four eggs cleanly on the edge of the pan, open just above the surface of the water and slide them smoothly into the pan. Place over a gentle heat so that the water does no more than tremble and cook for 2½ minutes. Take out the eggs one at a time with a skimmer and plunge for a few moments into a bowl of cold water. Trim away the loose pieces of egg white round the edges with a small knife and drain the eggs on a cloth. Transfer them to a dish and keep them on one side.

2 Melt the butter in a small saucepan, add the flour and cook for 5 minutes without allowing it to brown. Gradually add the stock to the roux, season and simmer very gently for just under an hour.

3 Separate two egg yolks and mix them with the cream, gradually adding a third of the sauce. Pour this liaison into the remaining sauce and reduce over a high heat, stirring constantly until you have about 200 ml (⅓ pint) left. Transfer the sauce to a bowl to cool and when it is lukewarm, use it to coat the four poached eggs on both sides and then leave to cool until the sauce has set.

4 Break an egg onto a plate and beat it with salt and pepper and the arachide oil. Sieve the breadcrumbs onto a second plate. When the sauce has thoroughly cooled on the eggs, cut away the surplus with the point of a knife. Then dip the eggs carefully one by one in the 'anglaise', or beaten egg mixture, and roll them in the breadcrumbs.

5 Heat the vegetable purée.

6 A few minutes before serving, heat plenty of arachide or sunflower oil in a deep frying-pan until a blue haze rises, put in the eggs, cook for 2 minutes, then gently move the pan to and fro so that the eggs turn themselves over. When they are a nice golden colour all over, after about 2 minutes more, drain them on kitchen paper and salt them lightly. Divide the vegetable purée between four small porcelain or earthenware dishes and place the eggs on top.

Editor's note The vegetable purée used in this dish was christened in honour of the football team of St Étienne, who wear green and are also known as the Stéphanois.

Surprise Eggs

Oeufs à la fausse coque

For four people
Preparation time: 25 minutes
Cooking time: 15 minutes

Ingredients   12 fresh Italian plum tomatoes, about 1 kg (2¼ lb)
80 g (2¾ oz) spinach
4 eggs
100 g (3½ oz) butter
1 clove of garlic, peeled
salt, freshly-ground pepper
12 egg cups

Preparation

1   Italian plum tomatoes are best for this dish, since they are oval, and smooth-sided. Bearing in mind that they will be used instead of egg shells, choose them of an even shape and size. Cut the tops off the tomatoes two thirds of the way up and remove the pips and half the flesh with a teaspoon. Season lightly inside with salt and pepper and then stand them upright in a saucepan just large enough to hold them side by side.

2   Prepare and cook the spinach in the classic way (see page 220). Drain it thoroughly, press it lightly to remove excess water and chop it fairly coarsely.

3   Separate the eggs, putting the whites and yolks into two bowls, season both with salt and beat them lightly.

Cooking

4 Cut 30 g (1 oz) butter into little pieces, and put them inside the twelve tomatoes. Put them under a heated grill, or heated sala-mander, for about 12 minutes, until they are cooked but still firm enough to be stuffed.

5 While they are cooking, heat 20 g ($\frac{3}{4}$ oz) butter to a hazelnut brown in a small saucepan. Put in the spinach and heat it through, stirring it round with a fork with a clove of garlic spiked onto the prongs. Do not allow the spinach to brown.

6 A few minutes before serving, cook the eggs in the following way. Take two small heavy saucepans so that the eggs won't cook too fast, or, failing these, use a bain-marie, which will take longer. Melt 10 g (2 teaspoons) butter in one of the pans placed over a very low heat, pour in the egg whites and stir continuously to combine the parts that are starting to set with the unset parts. As soon as the eggs are thickening slightly, remove the pan from the heat and let the egg whites finish cooking in their own heat. Keep the pan in a warm place while you repeat the process with the egg yolks in the other pan. Then stir 15 g ($\frac{1}{2}$ oz) butter, cut into small pieces, into each of the egg preparations.

Finishing and serving

7 Put the tomatoes into the egg-cups and then fill the first four with the scrambled egg whites, the next four with the scrambled egg yolks and the last four with spinach. Each guest will have three eggs of different colours – white, yellow and green. Serve at once.

Baked Eggs 'Paoli'

Oeufs au plat Paoli

For four people
Preparation time: 10 minutes
Cooking time: 3 minutes

Ingredients   8 new laid eggs
60 g (2 oz) raw cured ham (Bayonne or prosciutto
     crudo)
250 ml (scant half pint) double cream
20 g ($\frac{3}{4}$ oz) butter
salt, pepper

1   Preheat the oven to 200° C/400° F/Mark 6. Cut the ham into fine dice. Separate the eggs one at a time, putting the whites into a mixing bowl and dividing the yolks between four plates, putting two on each. Mix the cream into the whites, season with salt and beat with a whisk for 30 seconds; add the diced ham.

2   Take four ovenproof china egg dishes, heat through gently and melt 5 g (1 teaspoon) butter in each. When they are hot divide the egg white mixture between them and put them into the oven for one minute.

3   Slide out the ovenrack and slip two egg yolks into each dish. Give each a good turn of the peppermill, but don't salt them, and return to the oven for 2 minutes.

* Because the eggs are served in the same dishes, they will continue to cook in their own heat after they have come out of the oven. They should therefore be prepared at the last minute.

Editor's note   Many of Paoli's paintings hang on the walls of Les Frères Troisgros.

Fish

Troisgros Salmon Escalopes with Sorrel

Escalopes de saumon à l'oseille Troisgros

For four people
Preparation time: 40 minutes
Cooking time: 40 seconds for the salmon,
 10 minutes for the sauce

Ingredients
900 g (2 lb) fresh middle cut of salmon
80 g (2¾ oz) fresh sorrel
2 shallots
500 ml (scant pint) fish fumet (page 32)
4 tablespoons dry white wine (for instance, Sancerre)
2 tablespoons white Vermouth
400 ml (⅔ pint) double cream
40 g (1½ oz) butter
juice of ½ lemon
arachide oil
salt, freshly-ground pepper

(see colour illustration opposite page 81)

Preparation

1 Remove the two fillets from the backbone of the salmon with a sharp flexible knife, and remove the skin. With a pair of tweezers, extract the tiny bones from the middle of the flesh; you can detect them by running your fingertips against the grain of the flesh. Cut each fillet in half horizontally to make four escalopes of 140 g (5 oz) each. Oil two sheets of greaseproof paper, slide the escalopes between them and flatten them gently to an even thickness with a steak beater.

2 Trim the sorrel, removing the stalks and tough central fibres, wash it and tear the largest leaves into two or three pieces. Chop the shallots finely.

Cooking

3 Put the fish fumet, white wine, Vermouth and chopped shallots into a sauté pan, place it over the heat and reduce until you have a glistening syrup which is almost a glaze. Add the cream and let it boil until the sauce is slightly thickened. Throw in the sorrel and, after 25 seconds, take the pan off the heat and incorporate the butter in small pieces shaking the pan to and fro to emulsify the sauce, (don't use a whisk as this would break up the sorrel). Finish the sauce by adding a few drops of lemon juice, salt and pepper.

4 Heat a large frying-pan, without fat if it is a non-stick pan, or with a very little oil if it is the ordinary kind. Season the escalopes with salt and pepper on their least presentable side and put in the pan with the seasoned side down. After 25 seconds turn them over and cook on the other side for 15 seconds. The salmon must be under-cooked so that it remains succulent.

Serving

5 Spoon the sauce over the bottom of four large heated plates. Blot the surface of the escalopes with a cloth or kitchen paper to remove any oil from the surface and place them on top, with the best side uppermost. Sprinkle sparingly with fine salt.

* This dish cannot be kept waiting and should be prepared at the last moment.

Salt Cod 'Berchoux'

Feuillée de morue Berchoux

For four people
Preparation time: 45 minutes
Cooking time: 25 minutes

Ingredients   700 g (1 lb 9 oz) salt cod
2 anchovy fillets
half a clove of garlic, finely chopped
150 ml ($\frac{1}{4}$ pint) olive oil
juice of half a lemon
freshly-ground pepper
50 g (1$\frac{3}{4}$ oz) truffles (optional)

Preparation

1 Choose fine new season's fish, thick and white. Place a rack in the bottom of a large bowl, cut the fish into four and leave it to soak on the rack, covered with cold water for 48 hours, with the skin side up. Change the water three or four times.

Cooking

2 Cut the anchovy fillets into tiny dice. Set the olive oil on the edge of the stove to become lukewarm. To poach the fish, put the pieces into 2 litres ($3\frac{1}{2}$ pints) cold water, heat slowly and, as soon as it begins to boil, turn the heat right down so that the water barely trembles and leave for 15 minutes. Then put the fish in a sieve, remove the skin and bone and flake it up with your fingers.

3 Heat half a glass of water in a tinned copper pan and carefully put in the flakes of fish. Remove from the heat and incorporate the warm olive oil and the lemon juice drop by drop, shaking the pan continuously for 7 to 8 minutes. Don't allow the temperature to rise above 50° C/100° F. The mixture will thicken but if it looks as if it might separate (the olive oil won't amalgamate with the fish) add a little lukewarm water. Finally, add the anchovies and the finely-chopped garlic to the creamy sauce and a generous turn of the peppermill.

* Serve in a deep round dish with baked potatoes.

* For a richer dish, you can decorate the top with slices of truffle dipped in olive oil.

Editor's note   This dish is named after the poet Joseph Berchoux (1765–1839), born near Roanne and well known for his book on gastronomy which was published in 1800.

Fillets of Freshwater Perch Citronnelle

Filets de perche citronnelle

For four people
Preparation time: 1 hour
Cooking time: 20 minutes

Ingredients
3 lemons
4 perch weighing 400 g (14 oz) each
20 g ($\frac{3}{4}$ oz) sugar
2$\frac{1}{2}$ tablespoons wine vinegar
500 ml (scant pint) fish fumet (page 32)
50 g (1$\frac{3}{4}$ oz) butter
salt, freshly-ground pepper

1   Peel the lemons 'à vif' with a small knife, removing zest and pith and leaving the flesh completely exposed. Slide the knife between the flesh and inner membranes to separate the segments.

2   Have the perch filleted by the fishmonger, skin them, flatten them lightly with a steak beater and season with salt and pepper. Then roll each fillet round a segment of lemon and secure it with a wooden toothpick.

3   Melt the sugar in the vinegar in a small saucepan and cook gently until you have a clear caramel. Add the fish fumet, bring to the boil and allow to cool.

4   Butter a shallow saucepan, arrange the fish in it and cover with the fumet. Add the rest of the lemon segments, cover the pan and simmer for 15 minutes.

5   Take out the fish and lemon, place on a serving dish, cover with a plate and keep hot. Reduce the cooking liquid until you have six tablespoons of syrupy sauce, then add the remaining butter, cut in small pieces, and whisk to emulsify the sauce. Taste for seasoning.

6   Remove the toothpicks and serve the fish and lemon segments lightly coated with the hot sauce.

Red Mullet with Beef Marrow

Filets de rouget à la moelle de boeuf

For four people
Preparation time: 30 minutes
Cooking time: 10 minutes

Ingredients

120 g (4½ oz) beef marrow
6 red mullet, weighing 200 g (7 oz) each
a little flour
3 shallots, finely chopped
2½ tablespoons arachide oil
120 g (4½ oz) butter
200 ml (⅓ pint) red Burgundy
2 tablespoons fresh tomato sauce (page 39)
20 g (¾ oz) salt-cod salt (page 94) or coarse salt
salt, freshly-ground pepper

A day in advance

1 Ask the butcher for two fine, firm pieces of beef marrow and soak them in cold water for 12 hours.

Preparation and cooking

2 Drain the marrow and cut into rounds 1 cm ($\frac{1}{2}$ in) thick. Clean, scale and gut the red mullet and remove the fillets cutting along either side of the bone with a sharp knife. Wipe them with a cloth, season them with salt and pepper and dust them with flour, tapping them to shake off the excess, and put them on a board.

3 Put the slices of marrow carefully into a small saucepan, cover with 500 ml (scant pint) cold salted water, and take off the heat as soon as the liquid starts to tremble.

4 Heat the oil and 30 g (1 oz) butter in a frying-pan. When it is beginning to foam, put in the fish, skin side down, and cook for 2 minutes on each side, shaking the pan from time to time to prevent them from sticking. When they are cooked, put the fish, skin side up, on a serving dish and keep warm.

5 Sweat the shallots for 2 minutes in butter in the same frying-pan. Deglaze with the burgundy, add the fresh tomato sauce and reduce until you have 8 tablespoons of sauce. Take off the heat and whisk in 90 g ($3\frac{1}{2}$ oz) butter in small pieces. Taste for seasoning, adding a generous quantity of pepper.

Serving

6 Put the fillets on four large heated plates, coat them lightly with the sauce, and decorate with the rounds of hot marrow. Sprinkle each one with a pinch of salt-cod salt or coarse salt.

Marine 'Leg of Lamb' with Fresh Noodles

Gigot de mer braisé aux nouilles fraîches

For four people
Preparation time: 1 hour
Cooking time: 45 minutes

Ingredients
1 monkfish or angler fish tail weighing 800 g (1 lb 12 oz)
5 tomatoes
20 g ($\frac{3}{4}$ oz) butter
1 carrot
1 onion
a bouquet garni
5 tablespoons dry white wine
5 tablespoons double cream
a pinch of saffron
120 g ($4\frac{1}{2}$ oz) fresh noodles (tagliatelle)
3 cloves of garlic, peeled
salt, freshly-ground pepper

1   Skin the fish and cut off the fins. Make six small incisions at regular intervals with a small vegetable knife and stud with the cloves of garlic cut in two lengthwise. Season it with salt and pepper.

2   Plunge the tomatoes into boiling water, refresh under cold running water, skin them, then cut them in half and squeeze out the pips and excess moisture in the palm of your hand. Cut them into small even dice. Slice the carrot into rounds and cut the onion into quarters.

3   Heat the butter in a saucepan just large enough to hold the fish, fry the fish for 10 minutes over a brisk heat and surround with the sliced carrot and onion and the bouquet garni. Cover the pan and allow to simmer for 20 minutes, then add the white wine and cook for a further 25 minutes, basting frequently.

4   Add the cream and bring back to the boil. Carefully transfer the fish to a serving dish and strain the sauce through a fine conical sieve into a small saucepan. Add the saffron and the diced tomatoes and let it reduce over a low heat to a lightly thickened sauce. Taste for seasoning. Preheat the oven to 220°C/425°F/Mark 7.

5   Cook the noodles in plenty of salted water, keeping them 'al dente' or firm to the bite. Seven or eight minutes should be enough. Drain them in a colander.

6   Transfer the noodles to a long deep heated dish, arrange the fish in the middle, heat for 30 seconds in the oven and coat with the boiling sauce.

* The fish can be carved quite easily by following the line of the backbone.

Editor's note   The dense flesh of monkfish takes longer to cook than other varieties. If using, say, halibut or turbot, the cooking time can be cut by at least half.

Whiting 'Hôtel des Platanes'

Merlan 'Hôtel des Platanes'

For four people
Preparation time: 30 minutes
Cooking time: 12 minutes

Ingredients

4 whiting, weighing 300 g (10½ oz) each
150 ml (¼ pint) milk
flour
150 g (5¼ oz) button mushrooms
2 medium onions, chopped
100 g (3½ oz) butter
juice of ¼ lemon
salt, freshly-ground pepper

1   Choose four bright-eyed whiting, clean and gut them and trim the tails and fins with a pair of scissors. Wash them and dry them with a cloth. Make small incisions of 5 mm ($\frac{1}{4}$ in) every 2 cm ($\frac{3}{4}$ in) on both sides of the fish and season them with salt and pepper. Then dip them in milk and roll them in flour.

2   The mushrooms should be fresh, firm and white. Trim away the ends of the stalks, wash them quickly in water, clean and dry them in a cloth. Chop them coarsely.

3   Preheat the oven to 230° C/450° F/Mark 8. Cook the onions to a pale golden colour with 25 g (1 oz) butter in a small saucepan, add the mushrooms and let them cook, stirring constantly. Remove from the heat as soon as the moisture has evaporated.

4   Heat 50 g ($1\frac{1}{2}$ oz) butter in a frying-pan and, when it is hazelnut brown, put in the whiting. Cook for 4 minutes each side and then transfer to the hot oven for 4 minutes.

5   Just before serving, arrange the whiting carefully in a serving dish. Put the remaining 25 g (1 oz) of butter into a frying-pan and, when it is foaming, put in the mushroom mixture and fry to a nice golden colour, stirring constantly. Place on top of the whiting, sprinkle with lemon juice and serve immediately.

* This dish must not be kept waiting, and should be cooked just before you want to eat it.

Editor's note   The original name of the Troisgros restaurant at Roanne was the Hôtel des Platanes – plane trees still grow in front of the hotel.

Navarin of Lobster

Navarin de homard

For four people
Preparation time: 1 hour 30 minutes
Cooking time: 30 minutes

Ingredients   2–3 live female lobsters weighing 1·8 kg (4 lbs)
  altogether
2 shallots, ⎫
1 carrot, ⎬ cut into mirepoix dice
80 g (2¾ oz) butter
5 tablespoons arachide oil
1½ tablespoons cognac
5 tablespoons dry white wine
200 ml (⅓ pint) fish fumet (page 32)
2 tomatoes
1 tablespoon tomato purée
a bouquet garni
5 tablespoons double cream
salt, freshly-ground pepper

the vegetables:
150 g (1¾ oz) haricots verts
80 g (2¾ oz) petits pois
2 carrots
2 turnips
2 potatoes
coarse salt

1   The lobsters should feel heavy and have their eggs underneath
– take these off and put them in a bowl. Hold each lobster firmly
on a chopping board and cut off the tail with a large knife at the
point where the tail joins the head. Split the head in two down the
middle and carefully remove the small sac of grit. Extract the green
coral from the head and add to the lobster eggs in the bowl. Detach
the two large claws and crack them with the back of a heavy knife.
Season the lobster with salt and pepper and place it on a board.

2   To prepare the vegetables, skin, deseed and chop the tomatoes
and put them aside for the sauce. Cook the beans and the peas separately in a copious amount of salted water so that they remain green
and crisp. 'Turn' the carrots, turnips and potatoes into the shape
of cloves of garlic with a small sharp knife, cutting each vegetable
into 8 pieces, and cook them separately in boiling salted water. (See
illustration of the coupe-jarret opposite page 224 in which some
of the vegetables have been trimmed in this shape.)

3   Heat 20 g ($\frac{3}{4}$ oz) butter and the oil in a deep sauté pan until a
blue haze rises, and put in the pieces of lobster. Keep the pan over
a fairly brisk heat and turn the pieces of lobster until they have
become a fine red colour. Add the mirepoix of shallots and carrot,
sprinkle on the cognac and let it evaporate. Then add the white wine,
the fish fumet, the chopped tomatoes, the tomato purée and the bouquet garni. Bring to the boil and simmer for 15 minutes.

4   Take out the pieces of lobster with a fork, keep the tails and claws
warm and break up the head shells in a blender. Add them to the
liquid and let it boil for 10 minutes. Mash the lobster eggs and the
coral in the bowl with 60 g (2 oz) butter and add this liaison to the
sauce, which will turn a deep vermilion. Then pour in the cream and
boil for 3 minutes. Check the seasoning and strain through a fine
conical sieve.

5   Remove the lobster flesh from the tails and cut it into rounds.
Do the same with the claws but cut the meat into small dice. Add
to the sauce together with the carrots, turnips and potatoes. Heat
through without boiling.

6   Arrange the navarin in a deep dish and strew the beans and peas
on top.

Six-fish 'Ajano'

Panaché aux six poissons 'ajano'

For six people
Preparation time: 1 hour
Cooking time: 10 minutes

Ingredients 3 red mullet, each weighing 200 g (7 oz)
1 sea bass weighing 600 g (1 lb 5 oz)
1 sea bream weighing 800 g (1 lb 12 oz)
1 rascasse weighing 800 g (1 lb 12 oz)
3 weevers, each weighing 150 g (5¼ oz)
1 brill weighing 700 g (1 lb 9 oz)
3 carrots
3 turnips
100 g (3½ oz) French beans, broken into short
   lengths
50 g (1¾ oz) petits pois, shelled
2 tomatoes
1 shallot
240 g (8½ oz) butter
250 ml (scant half pint) dry white wine
juice of ½ lemon
flat-leaved or 'continental' parsley
salt, freshly-ground pepper

1 Make sure that the fish are fresh and ask the fishmonger to fillet them, leaving the skin on except in the case of the brill. Cut the fillets into small steaks of about 35 g ($1\frac{1}{4}$ oz) – there will be six for each person, one piece of each fish.

2 Peel the carrots and the turnips, and cut them into little sticks about 3 cm (1 in) long and then trim them into the shape of cloves of garlic, 30 of each vegetable. Cook them separately in boiling salted water, keeping them fairly firm. Cook the haricots verts and the petits pois in the same way. Plunge the tomatoes into boiling water to skin them, squeeze out the pips, cut the flesh evenly into small cubes and season them with salt and pepper. Chop the shallot finely.

3 Sprinkle the chopped shallot over the bottom of a large buttered sauté pan. Season the fish with salt and pepper and place each variety in turn, skin side upwards, in the pan. Pour on the white wine, bring to the boil, cover the pan and simmer gently for 5 minutes.

4 Transfer the cooking liquid from the fish to a separate saucepan, reduce it to half its volume and then, over a brisk heat, incorporate the butter in small pieces, whisking vigorously, until you have a smooth sauce. Taste for seasoning and add the lemon juice and the parsley leaves.

5 Reheat the vegetables (carrots, turnips, beans and peas) in a pan of boiling salted water. Have ready six large heated plates and arrange on each, in the shape of a star, the six varieties of fish, alternating the colours. Coat lightly and rapidly with the very hot sauce. Drain the vegetables and arrange them prettily on top of the fish, scattering the diced raw tomatoes on top.

Editor's note The 'ajano' of the title is a pun on Pierre Troisgros' answer to a customer's query about this recipe: he told him it was created by little Jean – 'à Jeannot'.

Thornback Skate with Oil and Vinegar

Raie bouclée à l'huile et au vinaigre

For four people
Preparation time: 20 minutes
Cooking time: 20 minutes

Ingredients
for the skate:
1 wing of skate weighing 1 kg (2¼ lb)
1 onion, finely sliced
1 carrot, finely sliced
10 g (¼ oz) whole peppercorns, coarsely crushed
a bouquet garni
5 tablespoons distilled vinegar
20 g (¾ oz) coarse salt

for the sauce:
½ teaspoon fine salt
a pinch of pepper
4 tablespoons wine vinegar
160 ml (¼ pint) olive oil
30 g (1 oz) whole coriander seeds
½ shallot
a few flat parsley leaves

for the garnish:
4 long waxy potatoes boiled in their skins

1   Choose the wing of a medium-sized thornback skate. Cut off about 2 cm (1 in) of the thin part at the edge of the wing and then divide the wing into four pieces of approximately equal size. Rinse thoroughly to remove all the slime from the skin.

2   Put the skate in a large saucepan and cover with 1 litre ($1\frac{3}{4}$ pints) water. Add the onion and carrot, the crushed peppercorns and the bouquet garni, the distilled vinegar and the coarse salt. Bring to the boil and, as soon as the liquid begins to tremble, cover the pan, take it off the heat and let it finish cooking for 20 minutes.

3   For the sauce, put the salt, pepper and wine vinegar in a bowl. Whisk in the oil gradually and add the coriander and the shallot.

4   Take out the pieces of skate one by one with a fork, being careful not to break them, and put them on a board. Skin them on both sides with a knife and put them on a heated serving dish. Peel the hot potatoes, cut into slices of 1 cm ($\frac{1}{2}$ in) and arrange them round the skate. Coat lightly with the sauce and sprinkle the parsley leaves over the top. Serve at once.

John Dory with Potatoes

Saint-Pierre à la boulangère

For four people
Preparation time: 30 minutes
Cooking time: 1 hour 5 minutes

Ingredients

1 John Dory weighing 1·5 kg (3 lb 6 oz)
1·5 kg (3 lb 6 oz) waxy potatoes
6 large onions
1 clove of garlic
1 litre (1¾ pints) poultry stock (page 27)
200 g (7 oz) butter
1 branch of fresh thyme
salt, freshly-ground pepper

1 Choose a fish at the peak of freshness and clean it by making a small incision in its side and running cold water through the gills to wash out the inside. Cut off the fins and the end of the tail with a pair of fish scissors. Wash and wipe the fish and season with salt and pepper.

2 If possible, choose a long, waxy variety of potato which will remain firm when cooked. Peel and wash the potatoes and slice evenly into very thin rounds. Slice the onions finely after cutting them in half downwards and removing the root end. Chop the clove of garlic finely.

3 Preheat the oven to 160° C/300° F/Mark 2. Bring the stock to the boil. Set 150 g (5 oz) butter to melt in a small pan. Melt 50 g (2 oz) butter in a frying-pan, and soften the onions, without browning, for 20 minutes.

4 Spread the onions in the bottom of an ovenproof dish large enough to hold the fish, add the chopped garlic and place the John Dory on top. Cover with the potatoes and pour on the boiling stock and the melted butter. Sprinkle with the thyme, rubbing the branch between your hands, and cover the whole surface with a sheet of greaseproof paper. Cook in the oven for 45 minutes.

5 Take the dish out of the oven and, if the stock has not been completely absorbed by the potatoes, pour it into a small saucepan, let it reduce until it becomes syrupy and then spoon it over the top. Serve in the dish in which it was cooked.

Grilled Sole with Chives

Sole à la ciboulette

For four people
Preparation time: 30 minutes
Cooking time: 20 minutes

Ingredients 4 sole weighing 350 g (12½ oz) each
100 g (3½ oz) day-old white bread, crusts removed
100 g (3½ oz) butter
chives
200 ml (⅓ pint) fish fumet (page 32)
5 tablespoons dry white wine
2 tablespoons dry white Vermouth
1 shallot, chopped
500 ml (scant pint) double cream
1 teaspoon tomato purée
juice of ½ lemon
salt, pepper

1   Rub the bread through a wire sieve. Clarify 75 g (2½ oz) butter. Cut up the chives with scissors. Preheat the oven to 200°C/400°F/Mark 6.

2   To prepare the sole, remove the dark skin from each fish, (or have it done for you by the fishmonger), scale the white side and cut off the head diagonally. Trim the tail and season with salt and pepper.

3   Put the clarified butter in a large oval, ovenproof dish. Dip the soles in the butter and then coat the white sides with the fine bread-crumbs. Put a little of the fish fumet in the bottom of the dish and put in the fish with the breadcrumbed sides uppermost, being careful not to get the breadcrumbs wet. Cook in the oven for 15 minutes and finish off under the grill to give the fish a nice golden colour. Take out the soles and remove the little bones on either side of the fish.

4   Boil the white wine, Vermouth, the remaining fish fumet and the shallot together with the tomato purée until almost completely reduced. Add the cream and bring to the boil to obtain a lightly thick-ened sauce. Strain through a fine conical strainer and work up with the rest of the butter. Add a squeeze of lemon juice and taste for salt and pepper.

5   Heat the soles in the oven, divide the sauce between four large plates, sprinkle with the chives and put the fish on top.

Chicken Turbot with Cucumber

Filets de turbotin aux concombres

For four people
Preparation time: 35 minutes
Cooking time: 30 minutes approximately

Ingredients
1 medium cucumber
1 chicken turbot weighing 1·3 kg (2 lb 14 oz)
2 shallots
200 ml ($\frac{1}{3}$ pint) dry white wine
500 ml (scant pint) double cream
juice of $\frac{1}{4}$ lemon
1 tomato
parsley, coarsely chopped
butter
salt, freshly-ground pepper

Ten to twelve hours in advance

1 Choose a long firm cucumber. Cut off the two ends and cut into
three short lengths. Peel each piece and cut downwards into thin
slices, discarding the pips. Then slice into julienne strips and leave
to soak in a bowl of cold water for 10 to 12 hours.

The turbot

2 If the fishmonger has not prepared the fish, fillet it in the following way. Using a long narrow-bladed knife, cut a line down the middle of the back from the base of the head to the tail. Through this incision feel the backbone with the knife blade and then slide the blade horizontally under the fillets to detach the flesh close to the bones. Do the same on the other side of the fish. You will end up with four fillets, two large and two small. Lift off the skin, both dark and white, and then cut the larger fillets into four and the smaller into two. This will give you twelve lozenge-shaped pieces of more or less the same size.

Cooking

3 To prepare the fumet, break up the head, backbone and tail of the fish roughly with a cleaver, put in a saucepan with 300 ml ($\frac{1}{2}$ pint) water and bring to the boil. Cook for 20 minutes and strain through a fine conical strainer. Chop the shallots finely.

4 Butter the bottom of a long ovenproof dish, put in the finely chopped shallots, season the pieces of turbot with salt and pepper and lay them side by side on top. Add the white wine and the warm fumet and cover with a sheet of buttered foil. Put the dish on the heat, bring to the boil and poach gently for 6 minutes.

5 Remove the dish from the heat, pour the cooking liquid into a small saucepan and reduce by three quarters of the volume. Add the cream and bring to the boil to reduce the sauce again. Let it simmer until you have about 200 ml ($\frac{1}{3}$ pint) sauce, then season with salt and pepper and add the lemon juice. Peel the tomato, squeeze out the pips and chop the flesh evenly into small cubes, drain the cucumber and plunge both into boiling salted water for 1 minute. Drain and add to the sauce.

Serving

6 Remove the buttered foil from the oven dish and make sure that there is no liquid left. Then coat the fish lightly with the sauce, arranging the cucumber and tomato on top. Simmer for 1 minute over the heat, strew with a very little chopped parsley and serve straight from the dish.

Mackerel with Scallops

Maquereaux Saint-Jacques

For four people
Preparation time: 45 minutes
Cooking time: 18 minutes

Ingredients

4 freshly-caught mackerel
8 live scallops
half a carrot
2 tomatoes
a clove of garlic
2 shallots
60 g (2 oz) butter
32 coriander seeds
5 tablespoons dry white wine
juice of half a lemon
2–3 sprigs of parsley, coarsely chopped
salt, freshly-ground pepper

1 Make sure the mackerel are at the peak of freshness – they should have shining eyes and rosy gills. Remove the gills and fins, clean and gut the fish and wash them in plenty of cold water. Using a narrow-bladed knife, cut along either side of the backbone from the inside of the fish to detach the flesh, cut through the bone with scissors at each end and remove it. Make four evenly-spaced slashes in the flesh on one side of the fish, and season with salt and pepper.

2 If possible, obtain live scallops and prepare them as described in step 1 of the following recipe. Cut them in half horizontally, season and insert them in the incisions in the mackerel, leaving them projecting a little out of the fish.

3 Preheat the oven to 200°C/425° F/Mark 7. Cut the carrot into mirepoix dice, skin, deseed and chop the tomatoes, and chop the garlic and shallot finely. Melt the 20 g ($\frac{3}{4}$ oz) butter in a gratin dish large enough to hold the four mackerel. Put in the vegetables, together with the coriander, let them soften over a medium heat for 2 minutes. Put the mackerel into the dish, pour on the white wine and the lemon juice and dot with the rest of the butter – 40 g ($1\frac{1}{2}$ oz) – cut into small pieces. Cover with a sheet of buttered greaseproof paper and bring to the boil.

4 Cook for 18 minutes in the hot oven. At the end of the cooking time, the sauce should be like a syrup, lightly glazing the fish. If it is too thin, pour the liquid into a small saucepan and allow to reduce until there are 8 tablespoons of sauce left.

5 Taste for seasoning, coat the fish lightly with the sauce and sprinkle with coarsely-chopped parsley. Serve immediately.

Steamed Scallops with Sauvignon Sauce

Coquilles Saint-Jacques à la vapeur

For four people
Preparation time: 30 minutes
Cooking time: 6 minutes

Ingredients 4 kg (8¾ lb) scallops in their shells (approximately 700 g (1½ lbs) without shells)
150 g (5¼ oz) butter
4 tablespoons vegetables from a court-bouillon (page 33)
5 tablespoons dry white wine (for instance, Sauvignon)
lemon juice
parsley
salt, freshly-ground pepper

---

1 Scallops are usually sold ready-prepared, but if possible try to obtain live scallops and open them yourself at the last minute, as follows. Slide the blade of a knife under the flat lid of the shell and cut through the muscle by which it is attached. With a spoon carefully scoop out the scallop attached to the hollow shell. Separate the white part, or 'noix', and the orange part, or coral, rejecting the frilly outer membranes, and wash them in plenty of water to remove all traces of sand; drain and cut the white part in half, horizontally.

2 Take a double boiler, steamer or couscoussier and butter the wire rack which fits inside. Put the scallops, seasoned with salt, and the vegetables from the court-bouillon on the rack, dot with nuts of butter and pour on the white wine. Cover the pan, place it on the heat and, as soon as it shows signs of boiling, take it off and let it stand in a warm place for 5 minutes. Then take off the lid and boil rapidly for one minute to emulsify the butter and wine.

3 Just before serving, remove the scallops and add a few leaves of parsley and some drops of lemon juice to the sauce. Divide the scallops between four soup plates, remove the rack from the pan and coat them lightly with the sauce.

Poultry and Game

Duckling with Blackcurrants

Canette aux baies de cassis

For four people
Preparation time: 1 hour
Cooking time: 20 minutes

Ingredients

2 female ducklings weighing 2 kg (4 lb 6 oz) each
1 tablespoon arachide oil
300 g (10½ oz) blackcurrants, fresh or frozen according to season
20 g (¾ oz) icing sugar
5 tablespoons wine vinegar
1 tablespoon blackcurrant jam
2 tablespoons crème de cassis (blackcurrant liqueur)
250 ml (⅓ pint) demi-glace (page 29)
80 g (2¾ oz) butter
salt, freshly-ground pepper

(*see colour illustration opposite page 112*)

The ducks

1 Preheat the oven to 220° C/425° F/Mark 7. Clean and truss the ducks and season with salt and pepper. Place in a large heavy saucepan or casserole, add the oil and cook for 20 minutes, turning so that they are evenly browned on all sides. Transfer to the hot oven and continue to cook for 25 minutes. Set aside to cool slightly.

2 Then turn the ducks onto their backs and untie the trussing string. Take off the legs and break at the joints. With a sharp knife, make an incision along the length of the breastbone as far as the wing joints which must then be severed. Pull the wings upwards to lift away the breasts. In the same way, carve off the 'filets mignons' (the long strips of flesh next to the breastbone). Cut off the parsons nose and chop up the carcases with a large, heavy knife.

The sauce

3 In a covered pan, cook the blackcurrants for 5 minutes with 3 tablespoons water and the sugar.

4 In another saucepan, reduce the vinegar and the blackcurrant jam to a caramel and deglaze with the crème de cassis. Add the demiglace, the duck carcases and the juice from the blackcurrants, bring to the boil and turn down the heat to its lowest position. Leave for about 20 minutes, skimming with a spoon. Strain the sauce through a fine conical strainer placed over a small saucepan, pressing the bones with a ladle to extract all the juices, and then whisk in the butter, in pieces, over a low heat. Add the blackcurrants, well drained, and check the seasoning, making sure that it is neither too sweet nor too salty.

Finishing and serving

5 Heat the oven to 220° C/425° F/Mark 7. Divide the duck legs in two at the top of the drumstick and cut each breast into four fillets removing the wings. Arrange the legs in the shape of a cross in the centre of the serving dish, with the fillets in a ring, slightly overlapping each other. Heat through in the hot oven for a few seconds and coat with the hot sauce. Decorate with the whole blackcurrants.

Poached Turkey with Vinaigrette

Dindonneau poché à la vinaigrette

For eight people
Preparation time: 1 hour
Cooking time: 2 hours

Ingredients

1 turkey weighing 2·75 kg (6 lb), fresh, not frozen
½ lemon
8 small carrots
8 small turnips
1 large celeriac
8 leeks
1 stick of celery
a sprig of thyme
½ bayleaf
½ cauliflower
1 teaspoon pale mustard
2 tablespoons wine vinegar
4 tablespoons walnut oil
2–3 sets chicken giblets
160 g (6 oz) truffles (optional)
fresh chervil
salt, freshly-ground pepper

Preparation

1 Clean the turkey. To make it easier to carve, remove the wishbone by freeing it from the surrounding flesh with the point of a small knife and pulling the bone out towards you. Make a slit on the insides of the lower legs and draw the tendons out of the drumsticks with a trussing needle. Remove the lower legs just below the joints. Truss the turkey and rub the skin with the half lemon.

2 Peel the carrots and the turnips. Cut the celery into sticks, set aside the white parts of the leeks, and make up a bouquet garni with the green leek leaves, the celery, the thyme and bayleaf. Trim the leaves from the cauliflower and divide into eight.

3 Make the sauce in a bowl. Mix the mustard, salt and pepper and the vinegar and gradually incorporate the walnut oil.

Cooking

4 Place the turkey in a large pan, add water to cover and surround it with the neck, the feet and, if possible, a few chicken giblets. Season with coarse salt and bring to the boil. Skim, add the bouquet garni and allow to simmer very gently.

5 After 1 hour 10 minutes, add the vegetables, except the cauliflower, bring back to the boil, cook for another 20 minutes and remove from the heat. Meanwhile cook the cauliflower in a separate saucepan for 10 minutes in some of the liquid from the turkey.

Serving

6 Untruss the turkey and present it on a large plate, surrounded by the vegetables. Serve the vinaigrette separately in a sauce-boat, with the thinly sliced truffles added at the last minute, or, if you are not using truffles, a good handful of chervil sprigs in the sauce.

* To carve the turkey, proceed as for a chicken. Detach the legs, using a kitchen fork as a lever, and cut the white meat parallel to the breastbone into the finest possible slices. Finish by detaching the wings.

Chicken with Chicory

Poulet aux chicons

For four people
Preparation time: 30 minutes
Cooking time: 45 minutes

Ingredients   1 chicken weighing 1·6 kg (3 lb 9 oz)
1 kg (2¼ lb) chicory
20 g (¾ oz) butter
500 ml (scant pint) double cream
juice of ¼ lemon
flour
salt, pepper

Preparation

1 Clean the chicken and take off the head and neck. Cut off the legs below the joint and extract the tendons through a small incision in the leg joint. With a knife, cut through the back of the chicken from head to tail and open it out flat, still joined along the breast-bone. Cut away the vertebral column and remove the small bones from the inside of the carcase.

2 Choose chicory roots of the same size, with good white leaves tightly furled. Trim the base and tip, and remove any wilted leaves. Then cut lengthwise into large julienne strips, wash and drain in a cloth.

Cooking

3 Season the flattened chicken with salt and pepper and dust it with the flour. Melt the butter in a large casserole, put in the chicken, skin side down, and let it brown, and then turn it over and brown the other side. Place the chicory around the bird, cover the pan and let it sweat for 15 minutes.

4 Pour in the cream, bring back to the boil and let it finish cooking gently. You can test it by pricking the joint of the leg with a trussing needle. If the liquid that runs out is still pink, cook for a few more minutes.

Finishing and serving

5 Season with more salt and pepper, if necessary, add the lemon juice and serve straight from the dish.

Editor's note If you are feeling frugal, half the quantities of cream and chicory would be plenty for four.

Chicken with Wine Vinegar

Poulet au vinaigre de vin

For four people
Preparation time: 30 minutes
Cooking time: 35 minutes

Ingredients   1 chicken weighing 1·5 kg (3 lb 6 oz)
1 carrot
1 onion
80 g (2¾ oz) butter
15 cloves of garlic, unpeeled
300 ml (½ pint) wine vinegar
1 tablespoon tomato purée
2 tomatoes
a bouquet garni
'perce-pierre' (pickled samphire) or chervil
salt, freshly-ground pepper

Editor's note   Samphire, fresh or pickled, is occasionally available in East Anglia on fish-stalls. Samphire is a marsh-plant looking rather like very thin asparagus, and having a succulent texture and salty flavour.

Preparation

1 Cut the chicken into four pieces, two legs, which you cut through at the joints, and two wings with the breast meat attached. Cut off the wing tips at the second joint. Cut through the breasts so that each makes two pieces, one with the first joint of the wings attached. Season with salt and pepper.

2 Make a stock with the carcase, wing tips, neck and feet (see note on page 27) of the chicken, together with the carrot and onion. Cover with water, cook for 30 minutes, strain and skim the surface to remove the fat.

Cooking

3 Take a casserole large enough to hold the eight pieces of chicken without overlapping, put it on the heat and melt $10\,g$ ($\frac{1}{4}$ oz) butter in it, then add the pieces of chicken, skin side down. Cook for 5 minutes without covering and turn the pieces over to brown on the other side. Add the cloves of garlic, cover the pan and leave to cook for 20 minutes.

4 Tilt the lid and tip the casserole to pour off the fat into a bowl. Deglaze the pan with the vinegar, let it reduce and then add the tomato purée, the tomatoes, skinned, deseeded and chopped, and the bouquet garni. Cover and cook for 10 minutes.

5 Take the pieces of chicken out of the pan and moisten the remaining juices with the stock. Let it boil until you have enough sauce to half cover the chicken pieces. Whisk in the remaining butter – $70\,g$ ($2\frac{1}{2}$ oz) – and strain through a conical strainer, pressing the garlic cloves to thicken the sauce and give it a very interesting flavour.

Serving

6 Pile the chicken pieces on a serving dish, coat with the sauce and sprinkle with 'perce-pierre' or chervil.

Chicken with Fresh Country Herbs

Poulet aux herbes de province

For four people
Preparation time: 30 minutes
Cooking time: 1 hour 10 minutes

Ingredients

1 chicken weighing 1·5 kg (3 lb 6 oz)
35 g (1¼ oz) parsley
15 g (½ oz) tarragon
a bunch of chervil
25 g (1 oz) basil
5 sprigs of mint
270 g (10 oz) butter
6 tablespoons lemon juice
a sprig of thyme
½ bayleaf
a sprig of rosemary
1 sage leaf
180 g (6½ oz) rice
salt, freshly-ground pepper

Editor's note   The French title of this recipe pokes fun at the exaggerated reputation of herbs from Provence – as good a result can be obtained with herbs from other regions.

1   Take the first five herbs, parsley, chervil, tarragon, basil and mint, and remove the stalks. Wash the herbs, drain and dry them in a cloth. Slice up a third of these herbs and mix thoroughly with 180 g (6½ oz) softened butter, adding salt and pepper and the lemon juice.

2   Singe and clean the chicken and place on its back with the breast towards you. Without tearing it, loosen the skin from the surface of the breast by sliding your fingers between the flesh and the skin. Make a gash along each side of the breast meat, inside the skin, which must remain intact, and fill with half the herb butter, spreading the rest under the skin. Truss the chicken and season inside and out with salt and pepper.

3   Melt the rest of the butter – 90 g (3¼ oz) – in an oval casserole, lay the chicken on its side and let it brown. Turn it onto the other side to brown, keeping an eye on its progress, and finally turn the chicken breast upwards. Surround it with all the remaining herbs including the thyme, bayleaf, rosemary and sage, cover the pan and cook very gently on the edge of the heat or over an asbestos plate for about 1 hour 10 minutes. Baste frequently throughout the cooking time so that the herbs are kept moist and don't burn.

4   Wash the rice in plenty of cold water in a sieve, then cook in a large saucepan of boiling salted water for 18 minutes. Cool under cold water for a second, drain in a sieve and keep hot.

5   Untie the trussing string from the chicken, remove the thyme, bayleaf, rosemary and sage, and place it on a hot plate, covered with the herb garnish. Turn the rice into a dish and moisten with 8 tablespoons of butter spooned from the surface of the pan juices. Season lightly with salt and return to the oven, covered with greaseproof paper.

6   Reduce and caramelise the pan juices in the bottom of the casserole without letting them burn and add 5 tablespoons water or more to produce a slightly greenish sauce. Reduce until you have 2 generous tablespoons per person.

7   Serve the chicken in a deep dish, covered with the herbs and coated lightly with the sauce. Serve the rice separately.

Pigeons with Garlic

Pigeons aux gousses d'ail en chemise

For four people
Preparation time: 30 minutes
Cooking time: 20 minutes

Ingredients   4 pigeons
100 g (3½ oz) butter
24 cloves garlic, unpeeled
10 g (¼ oz) foie gras (optional)
1½ tablespoons cognac
5 tablespoons poultry stock (page 27)
salt, freshly-ground pepper

(see colour illustration opposite page 113)

Preparation

1 Clean the pigeons and reserve the livers in a bowl. (The livers of pigeons, unlike those of other birds, do not contain the bitter gall bladder). Singe the birds and remove the neck where it joins the body. Slip 10 g ($\frac{1}{4}$ oz) butter into each pigeon and truss them, first cutting the nerve at the joint of the legs so that they do not curl up. Season with salt and pepper.

2 Separate the cloves of garlic but do not peel them. Press the foie gras through a sieve.

Cooking

3 Preheat the oven to 220° C/425° F/Mark 7. Heat the remaining butter in a heavy pan, put in the pigeons and brown them lightly on all sides. Surround with the cloves of garlic and cook for 20 minutes in the oven, basting frequently.

4 Put the pigeons on a plate in a warm place with 8 cloves of garlic and their cooking butter. In the same pan, sauté the pigeon livers with the remaining cloves of garlic, deglaze with the cognac and press livers and garlic through a sieve onto the foie gras.

5 Put the stock (or failing that, water) into the pan, bring to the boil and thicken with the garlic and liver purée. Untruss the pigeons, simmer for 2 to 3 minutes in the sauce and taste for seasoning.

Serving

6 Serve on a heated serving dish, lightly coated with the sauce and surrounded by the whole cloves of garlic.

* Serve with Gaufrette Potatoes (page 235).

Golden Squabs

Pigeonneaux sable doré

For four people
Preparation time: 45 minutes
Cooking time: 28 minutes

Ingredients   4 squabs (young pigeons)
3 teaspoons English mustard powder
600 ml (1 pint) dry white wine
fresh breadcrumbs
1 kg (2¼ lb) celeriac
150 g (5¼ oz) butter
1 tablespoon cognac
2 teaspoons Dijon mustard
salt, freshly-ground pepper

1   Clean the squabs, remove the necks, heads and feet, singe and truss them. Mix the powdered mustard with 1 tablespoon white wine, brush this onto the birds, then roll them in the breadcrumbs, pressing them in well. Melt 30 g (1 oz) butter, roll the squabs in this and bread-crumb them again. Preheat the oven to 220° C/425° F/Mark 7.

2   Peel the celeriac and cut into large olive shapes 4 cm (1½ in) long. Blanch them for 8 minutes in boiling salted water. Refresh in cold water and drain in a colander.

3   Melt the remaining butter – 120 g (4½ oz) – in a casserole large enough to hold the birds and vegetables. As soon as it starts to foam, put in the squabs, let them brown to a golden colour for 10 minutes in the hot oven and then surround with the celeriac. Cook for another 12 minutes, then take out the squabs and celeriac together with the cooking butter and breadcrumbs that have collected in the bottom of the pan, and keep them hot.

4   Deglaze the pan with the cognac and then with the rest of the wine and let it evaporate completely. Moisten with 3 tablespoons water, bring to the boil, add the Dijon mustard and put in the squabs, untrussed, together with the celeriac, breadcrumbs and but-ter; simmer for 2 to 3 minutes. Taste for seasoning.

5   Cut the birds in half, arrange on a plate surrounded by the celeriac and coat lightly with the sauce. The fried breadcrumbs in the sauce will look like golden sand.

Pigeon 'Agates' with Mint

Agates de palombes à la menthe

For four people
Preparation time: 30 minutes
Cooking time: 4 minutes

Ingredients

2 young wood pigeons
100 g ($3\frac{1}{2}$ oz) best quality lean streaky bacon
$\frac{1}{2}$ shallot
50 g ($1\frac{3}{4}$ oz) butter
1 tablespoon cognac
32 mint leaves
thyme, bayleaf, rosemary
2 g (pinch) pepper
salt

1 Pluck and clean the pigeons, bone them and put the breasts on one side, after taking off the skin. Reserve the carcases.

2 Cut the bacon into small cubes. Chop the shallot finely and sweat in a little butter without browning for 5 minutes.

3 Roll the butter into 32 little balls the size of a cherry stone and put them in the freezer.

4 Mince the bacon on the medium blade of the mincer or, better still, chop it in a food-processor and add the pigeon breasts a few seconds later. Chop finely, then put the meat in a bowl with the shallot, cognac and pepper, and mix together thoroughly. The bacon will probably provide enough salt but check the seasoning. (**Editor's note** This can be done by rolling some of this mixture into a ball and frying it. You can then taste the seasoning.)

5 Cover each butter ball with 10 to 15 g ($\frac{1}{3}$ to $\frac{1}{2}$ oz) of the farce, rolling them between your fingers, which you have moistened with cognac. Wrap each one in a mint leaf.

6 Put the pigeon carcases, the thyme, bayleaf and rosemary in the bottom of a steamer, cover with cold water, making sure that it comes to below the level of the rack, and put in the rack with the 'agates' arranged side by side on it. Put the pan over the heat, cover the steamer, bring to the boil and then cook for 4 minutes. Take out the 'agates' and eat at once.

* These can be served with drinks or as an entrée with tomato sauce (page 39).

Editor's note The 'palombes' specified in the original recipe are migratory doves, a great speciality in South-Western France, where they are trapped and netted as they fly overhead by an ancient method involving the use of hooded lure-doves. Very young plump wood pigeons would make a perfectly good substitute in this recipe.

Aiguillettes of Mallard with Wild Mushrooms

Aiguillettes de col-vert aux mousserons des prés

For four people
Preparation time: 1 hour
Cooking time: 18 minutes

Ingredients

2 plump mallards
10 g ($\frac{1}{3}$ oz) fresh foie gras
2$\frac{1}{2}$ tablespoons arachide oil
2$\frac{1}{2}$ tablespoons cognac
4 shallots
a bouquet garni
400 ml ($\frac{2}{3}$ pint) red Burgundy
250 ml (scant half pint) demi-glace (page 29)
or water
150 ml ($\frac{1}{4}$ pint) double cream
500 g (1 lb 2 oz) wild mushrooms (millers)
80 g (2$\frac{3}{4}$ oz) butter
a sprig of parsley, chopped
salt, freshly-ground pepper

The ducks

1 Choose young birds – you can tell their age by the flexibility of the beak. Pluck, singe and clean them, cut off the tail or parson's nose and truss them. Take out the liver, discarding the gall-bladder and the greenish parts surrounding it, and press through a sieve with the foie gras. Reserve the liver mixture in a cold place to use later as a liaison for the sauce.

2 Preheat the oven to 230°C/450°F/Mark 8. Season the ducks with salt and pepper and sprinkle with the arachide oil. Put them to cook in the oven in a roasting pan for 18 minutes. Then leave the ducks to rest for 1 hour. The flesh will relax and turn an even rosy pink.

3 When they have cooled, untie the trussing string, remove the legs from the ducks and, following the line of the breastbone, carve off the two fillets from each bird and the two 'filets mignons' which lie along the breast next to the bone. Keep the four wings on one side.

The sauce

4 Chop the necks, legs and carcases of the ducks with a cleaver and brown them in butter in a large saucepan. When they are a nice golden colour, drain off the fat and deglaze the pan with the cognac. Add 3 shallots, cut in quarters, the pepper and the bouquet garni and pour on the red wine and the demi-glace or water, adding more water if necessary to cover the bones. Bring to the boil and simmer for 1 hour.

5 Strain the stock through a conical strainer, clean the saucepan and pour back the stock. Allow to reduce, skimming frequently until you have 150 ml ($\frac{1}{4}$ pint) liquid left. Then pour in the cream, bring to the boil and add the liaison of livers, shaking and swirling the pan to emulsify the sauce. Taste for seasoning. The sauce is now ready and should not be allowed to boil again.

The mushrooms

6 Remove the stalks from the mushrooms and wash them briefly in two lots of water, but do not let them soak. Season them with a little salt and let them cook in their own juices in a covered pan for 2 minutes.

7 Drain them and then fry in 80 g ($2\frac{3}{4}$ oz) butter for a few minutes until lightly browned. At the last moment, add the remaining shallot, chopped, and the parsley.

Finishing and serving

8 Skin the larger duck fillets and cut each into 5 thin slices. Arrange them slightly overlapping in a ring, together with the 'filets mignons', round a large heated dish. Pile the mushrooms in the middle and place the four wings on top. Heat through for 20 seconds in the oven and then pour a thread of sauce over the duck breasts, serving the rest of the sauce in a hot sauce boat.

Woodcock 'Maître Richard'

Bécasse Maître Richard

For four people
Preparation time: 1 hour 30 minutes
Cooking time: 18 minutes

Ingredients
4 woodcock
80 g (2¾ oz) butter
40 g (1½ oz) foie gras
4 slices of white bread
2½ tablespoons cognac
⅓ of a bottle of full-bodied red wine, preferably
  Chambertin
5 tablespoons demi-glace (page 29)
2 strips of lemon peel
salt, freshly-ground pepper

The woodcock

1 Pluck the woodcock at the last minute but don't gut them. Take out the eyes, then fasten the thighs with the beak, passing it right through the body like a skewer. In this way, there will be no need to truss them. Season with salt and pepper.

2 Preheat the oven to 230°C/450°F/Mark 8. Heat the butter in a roasting pan of the right size to hold the woodcock and, as soon as it is foaming, turn the birds in it to seize them, then cook in the oven for 18 minutes, turning them over and basting them. They should be rosy pink, but not bloody.

The farce

3 Carefully remove the trail or innards of the birds with the back of a spoon and throw out the gizzard, which is easily recognisable as a little hard ball. In a mortar or, failing that, a mixing bowl, pound the entrails with the foie gras and season lightly with salt and pepper. Keep the birds warm.

The croûtons

4 Cut out of the bread four rectangular croûtons, 8 cm (3 in) by 4 cm (1¾ in) and 1 cm (½ in) thick. With a knife, mark out a smaller rectangle 6 cm (2¼ in) by 3 cm (1 in) on each croûton and then toast them. With the tip of a knife blade scrape out the crumb inside the rectangles you have marked, to give four little cases. Fill these with half the farce.

The sauce

5 Drain the cooking juices from the roasting pan into a bowl. Deglaze the pan with the cognac, add the red wine, demi-glace and strips of lemon peel and allow to evaporate almost completely. Then pour back the cooking juices, bring to the boil and incorporate the rest of the farce, shaking and swirling the pan to amalgamate the sauce. Taste for seasoning.

Finishing and serving

6 Split the woodcock in half, remove the breastbone and put the birds to simmer in the sauce for 2 minutes. Heat the croûtons in the oven and place the woodcock on top. Serve the strained sauce separately in a sauce boat.

* Finish the rest of the bottle of Chambertin with the dish.

* Woodcock should be hung by the feet; how long they should hang depends on the outside temperature but it should never be more than a week.

Editor's note Maître Richard was the Troisgros brothers' teacher at the Lucas-Carton restaurant in the Place de la Madeleine in Paris, where many famous chefs have served apprenticeships. This recipe is one of the most famous Lucas-Carton dishes.

Partridge with Green Lentils

Perdreaux aux lentilles vertes

For four people
Preparation time: 1 hour 30 minutes
Cooking time: 20 minutes

Ingredients   4 young partridge
100 g (3½ oz) small green lentils (lentilles du Puy)
1 carrot
2 onions
a bouquet garni
130 g (4⅓ oz) butter
1 tablespoon cognac
10 g (⅓ oz) foie gras
1 teaspoon strong pale mustard
5 tablespoons red wine
salt, coarse and fine, freshly-ground pepper

One day in advance

1   Soak the lentils in cold water.

Preparation and cooking

2   Drain the lentils and put them in a saucepan with twice their volume of water. Bring to the boil and remove the scum from the surface. Add the carrot, one onion and the bouquet garni, season with salt and cook gently so that the liquid is just shivering, checking from time to time to see if they are done.

3 The partridges, although they should obviously not be freshly shot, should be fresh and without any hint of being 'high'. Pluck and clean them, reserving the liver but discarding the gall-bladder, and singe them. Cut off the feet just below the leg joint, cut the neck close to the body, and pull the skin down over the neck cavity to cover the opening. Stuff each bird with 10 g ($\frac{1}{3}$ oz) butter and 3 or 4 grains of coarse salt. Truss them, keeping the legs close to the sides of the body. Preheat the oven to 230°C/450°F/Mark 8.

4 Heat 60 g (2 oz) butter in a roasting pan, roll the partridges in it and cook them in the oven for 20 minutes, basting two or three times. Take them out and keep in a warm place, reserving the butter and juices in the pan.

5 Chop the second onion and brown it lightly in 30 g (1 oz) butter in a small saucepan. Deglaze with the red wine and let it evaporate completely. Drain the lentils of all but a spoonful of their cooking liquid and add to the pan.

6 Sauté the seasoned livers for 1 minute in half the butter in which the partridges were cooked, deglaze the pan with the cognac and press through a sieve with the foie gras and the mustard. Reserve the mixture in a bowl, to be used later as a liaison for the sauce.

Finishing and serving

7 Add the liver mixture to the lentils and stir it in thoroughly, taste the sauce and add salt and pepper if necessary. Heat the partridges for a few minutes in the oven and remove the trussing strings.

8 Put the lentils in the bottom of a deep heated dish and place the partridges on top. Serve the rest of the cooking butter and juices from the roasting tin in a hot sauce boat.

Teal with Fresh Peaches

Sarcelles aux pêches

For four people
Preparation time: 45 minutes
Cooking time: 25 minutes

Ingredients

4 fresh teal
4 fresh yellow peaches
300 g (10½ oz) caster sugar
arachide oil
1 tablespoon cognac
1 tablespoon apricot jam
2½ tablespoons wine vinegar
juice of ½ lemon
200 ml (⅓ pint) demi-glace (page 29)
100 g (3½ oz) butter
icing sugar
salt, pepper

1   Pluck and clean the teal, cut off the parson's nose, singe and truss them. Preheat the oven to 230°C/450°F/Mark 8.

2   Skin the peaches, which will be easy if they are ripe; if not, plunge them in boiling water for one minute and then skin. Cut them in half, discard the stones and put the 8 halves to poach in 750 ml (1¼ pints) water, in which you have dissolved the caster sugar, for 5 minutes. Leave them in their syrup.

3   Season the teal, coat them with a little oil and roast in a casserole in the hot oven for 12 minutes. Take them out of the oven and let them rest for 30 minutes.

4   Pour the fat out of the casserole and deglaze it with the cognac. Add the jam and the vinegar and cook until caramelised. Then add the lemon juice and the demi-glace and allow to reduce for 5 minutes, skimming off any impurities that rise to the surface. Strain through a fine conical strainer and whisk in the butter in small pieces. The sauce should be smooth and glistening. Taste for seasoning.

5   Drain the peach halves, place them on a baking sheet, sprinkle with the icing sugar and put under the grill to heat through and give them a light golden glaze. Untruss the birds.

6   Place the four teal on a large heated serving dish, coat them lightly with the sauce and garnish with the glazed peaches.

* If teal are unavailable, this recipe can be made with any other wild duck.

Stuffed Rabbit 'Georgette Badaut'

Lapin farci 'Georgette Badaut'

For six people
Preparation time: 1 hour 30 minutes
Cooking time: 1 hour 10 minutes

Ingredients *for the stuffing:*
100 g (3½ oz) smoked streaky bacon
200 g (7 oz) mushrooms
200 g (7 oz) cooked spinach
2 shallots
80 g (2¾ oz) butter
5 g (a good pinch) salt, 2 g (a pinch) of freshly-
  ground pepper

for cooking the rabbit:
1 rabbit weighing 2·5 kg (5 lb 10 oz)
2 tablespoons pale Dijon mustard
50 g (1¾ oz) butter
a large branch of fresh thyme
500 ml (scant pint) red Burgundy, preferably
  Pommard
3 shallots
250 ml (scant half pint) cream
salt, pepper

Editor's note This dish would not lose much if you decided to remove the head before cooking the rabbit: although our Victorian ancestors liked their rabbits and hares to be sitting lifelike on the serving dish, it is not guaranteed to go down well with everybody today.
Georgette Badaut is an ancient and venerable aunt of the Troisgros brothers.

Preparation

1 Cook the mushrooms in one tablespoon of water and 30 g (1 oz) butter in a covered saucepan for 5 minutes. Then make the stuffing. Cut the bacon into small lardons and brown them in a frying-pan. Chop the mushrooms and the spinach coarsely. Chop the shallots and soften in a little butter. Put all these ingredients into a bowl, add the salt and pepper and mix with the softened butter.

2 Prepare the rabbit as follows, or ask the butcher to do it. Cut off the fore and hind legs below the knee joints and skin the rabbit, keeping the head with ears intact but removing the eyes. Make a slit of 8 cm (3 in) along the belly and remove the innards. Keep the liver but be sure to get rid of the gall-bladder.

3 Put the rabbit on its back and, using a spoon, fill the inside with the stuffing. Sew up the belly with a trussing needle and thin string. Turn the rabbit over and truss in a crouching position, fastening the forelegs in place with a string passed through the top of the shoulders with the larding needle. Fasten the hindlegs in the same way. Season with salt and pepper and paint with the mustard, using a pastry brush to spread it evenly over the whole surface.

Cooking

4 Preheat the oven to 250° C/500° F/Mark 10. Heat a roasting pan, melt the butter in it and then roll the rabbit in the butter. Put in the oven. Heat one third of the red wine in a small saucepan. After about 10 minutes, lower the heat to 190° C/375° F/Mark 5 and baste frequently with the branch of thyme, dipped into the hot red wine. Cook for an hour, then remove the rabbit and keep it hot.

5 Chop the shallots and the liver and brown them lightly in the juices in the roasting pan. Deglaze with the rest of the wine and let it reduce, then add the cream and let it boil until the sauce has thickened and emulsified. Taste for seasoning.

Finishing and serving

6 Take off all the string from the rabbit and place on a long dish in a natural position. Coat it lightly with a little of the hot sauce and serve the rest separately in a sauce boat. Put a spoonful of stuffing from the rabbit on each of four hot plates. Carve off the hindlegs, detach the forelegs and slice the saddle. Divide the meat between the plates and coat with the sauce.

Rabbit Stew with Dried Apricots

Compote de lapin de garenne aux abricots secs

For four people
Preparation time: 1 hour 30 minutes
Cooking time: 50 minutes

Ingredients

1 young wild rabbit
250 ml (scant half pint) red Burgundy
5 tablespoons wine vinegar
2 cloves of garlic, unpeeled
a bouquet garni
150 g (5¼ oz) dried apricots
2½ tablespoons arachide oil
50 g (1¾ oz) butter
salt, freshly-ground pepper

Twelve hours in advance

1   Skin the rabbit, gut it and keep the liver, having removed the gall-bladder. Bone the saddle, legs and shoulders and cut the meat into cubes of 25 g (1 oz). Marinate them in an earthenware or porcelain dish with the wine, the vinegar, the garlic and the bouquet garni for 12 hours.

Preparation and cooking

2   Cut the apricots in half and soak them for 1 hour in cold water.

3   Remove the pieces of rabbit, the garlic and the bouquet garni from the liquid with a slotted spoon and dry them thoroughly in a cloth or kitchen paper. Heat the oil and half the butter in a fairly large casserole, put in the pieces of rabbit, season with salt and pepper and fry them to an even brown. Add the garlic and the bouquet garni, cover the pan and cook gently for 20 minutes.

4   Turn up the heat, take off the lid and add the marinade and the drained apricots. Stir until the liquid comes to the boil and then cover with a sheet of buttered greaseproof paper, placed on top of the meat. Put on the lid and cook for 20 minutes. Half way through the cooking add the liver cut in four pieces.

5   Retrieve the cloves of garlic, skin them, and pound them in a bowl with the cooked livers and the rest of the butter. Then add this liaison to the sauce, having removed the bouquet garni, and stir gently so that it is mixed in thoroughly. Taste for seasoning adding salt and pepper if necessary.

Serving

6   Arrange the pieces of rabbit and the apricots alternately in a deep round heated dish and pour the sauce over the top.

Hare Stewed in Ambierle Wine

Daube de lièvre au vin d'Ambierle

For five or six people
Preparation time: 1 hour
Cooking time: 5 hours

Ingredients 1 hare
2 bayleaves
4 fresh mint leaves
1 leaf of basil
1 sprig of thyme
5 cloves of garlic, peeled
2 tablespoons tomato purée
15 peppercorns, coarsely crushed
20 coriander seeds
750 ml (1¼ pints) Ambierle wine (côte roannaise)
100 g (3½ oz) streaky bacon
2 strips of lemon peel
2 strips of orange peel
coarse salt

One day in advance

1   Choose a hare under six months old, known as 'trois quarts' because it is from one of the first litters of the year. At this age, it should weigh between 2·4 and 2·9 kg (5 lb 6 oz and 6½ lb) and certainly not more than 3 kg (6 lb 12 oz). Skin and clean it, reserving the blood and the liver after discarding the gall-bladder.

2   Cut it into 18 pieces, cutting each hindleg into four, each foreleg into two, and the saddle into six. Put the pieces into a medium-sized enamelled iron casserole together with the herbs, the garlic, the tomato purée, the crushed peppercorns and the coriander seeds, and cover with the wine. Leave to marinate overnight in a cool place.

Preparation and cooking

3   Remove the rind and cut the bacon into large lardons, 3 cm (1 in) square and 5 mm (¼ in) thick. Cut the rind into small dice and blanch them with the lardons for 2 minutes in boiling water.

4   Cut the liver of the hare into 4 small escalopes. Chop the strips of lemon and orange peel roughly and blanch in boiling water.

5   Put the casserole, to which you have added the chopped blanched orange and lemon peel, over the heat and add a little coarse salt. Cover the pan hermetically with an upturned lid filled with cold water so that the drops of condensation fall back into the stew. Lower the heat and let it bubble steadily for 3 hours. Then add the lardons and the rind and cook for 2 hours more.

6   Five minutes before the end of the cooking time, skim the fat from the surface with a spoon and remove the herbs. Add the slices of liver and the blood of the hare and heat very gently for 5 minutes. Taste for seasoning.

Serving

7   Serve straight from the casserole accompanied by pasta, with or without truffles (page 252), in a separate dish.

Saddle of Venison with White Pepper

Selle de chevreuil panée au poivre blanc

For four people
Preparation time: 30 minutes
Cooking time: 40 minutes

Ingredients

1 saddle of roe-deer weighing about 1 kg (2¼ lb)
2 tablespoons virgin olive oil
15 g (½ oz) white peppercorns
50 g (1¾ oz) butter
2 tablespoons cognac
5 tablespoons dry white wine
5 tablespoons game stock (page 31)
150 ml (¼ pint) double cream
salt

Twelve hours in advance

1   The saddle is the part that lies between the top of the hindlegs and the first ribs. With a fine-bladed knife, take off the thin membrane which covers it, leaving the meat exposed, then place the saddle in a deep dish and roll it in the olive oil. Crush the peppercorns with an empty bottle and press them into the meat so that it is 'breadcrumbed' all over. Set aside in a cool place for 12 hours.

Cooking

2   Preheat the oven to 230°C/450°F/Mark 8. Heat the butter in a roasting pan, put in the saddle and cook in the oven for 35 to 40 minutes, basting frequently. Take it out and keep it hot on a serving dish, covered with a sheet of buttered greaseproof paper.

3   Drain off the cooking fat from the pan, deglaze the pan with the cognac and then the white wine and let it reduce by half. Then add the game stock (this can be replaced by good veal stock if necessary), bring to the boil, add the cream and reduce, stirring all the time. Pour in the juices that have run out of the saddle and taste for seasoning, adding salt if necessary. Don't, on any account, add any pepper!

Finishing and serving

4   Carve off the two large fillets from the bone of the saddle and cut them into 12 medallions. Then detach the two 'filets mignons' underneath the saddle and cut these into 8 thin escalopes.

5   Arrange the medallions in a ring round the outside of a serving dish and place the escalopes in the centre. Coat with the boiling sauce, including all the peppercorns which have fallen off during the cooking.

* Serve with Soufflé Chestnuts (page 246).

Wild Boar Cutlets 'Fructidor'

Côtes de marcassin 'fructidor'

For four people
Preparation time: 1 hour
Cooking time: 20 minutes

Ingredients
8 cutlets of wild boar, weighing about 1·6 kg (3 lb
   10 oz) altogether, trimmed
2 tablespoons arachide oil
½ onion
½ carrot
4 pears, weighing 600 g (1 lb 5 oz) altogether
170 g (6 oz) butter
sugar
4 apples, weighing 600 g (1 lb 5 oz) altogether
8 chestnuts
4 fine prunes, soaked overnight
2 shallots, chopped
3 tablespoons wine vinegar
4 tablespoons dry white wine
12 juniper berries, lightly crushed
salt, freshly-ground pepper

The Wild Boar

1 Ask your game merchant to prepare 8 cutlets from a young boar of 30 to 40 kg (66 to 88 lb). Get him to cut off excess fat, to remove the chine bone, leaving just the rib bone, and to beat the cutlets to flatten them slightly. Also get him to chop up the trimmings and bones for you.

The stock

2 Brown the trimmings and bones of boar in the arachide oil in a small saucepan, together with the onion and carrot, add 500 ml (scant pint) water and let it simmer gently for a good hour, adding more water as necessary to keep up the level. Strain through a conical strainer, skim off the fat and let it reduce until you have 150 ml ($\frac{1}{4}$ pint) liquid.

The fruit

3 Choose half ripe pears, peel them, cut them into four, discard the pips and 'turn' them into the shape of 16 large olives 3 cm (1 in) long. Put them into a saucepan large enough to hold them side by side, with 250 ml (scant half pint) water, 30 g (1 oz) butter and a pinch of sugar. Half cover the pan and cook until the fruit is glazed, in other words has turned golden with the caramelised sugar. Keep the pears firm and don't overcook.

4 The apples should be slightly underripe and are prepared in the same way as the pears. The length of cooking for both fruits depends on how ripe they are.

5 Plunge the chestnuts for 5 minutes in boiling water and peel them, removing the inner skins. Cook them gently for 20 minutes in a small covered saucepan, half filled with water, plus 20 g ($\frac{3}{4}$ oz) butter and a pinch of sugar.

6 Having soaked the prunes the previous day, put them to cook in water. As soon as it comes to the boil, take them out and drain, cut them in half and remove the stones and then fry gently in 20 g ($\frac{3}{4}$ oz) butter.

(*continued on the next page*)

Cooking

7   Heat 50 g (1¾ oz) butter in a frying-pan, season the boar cutlets and cook them gently on both sides, without letting them become dry, for 15 to 20 minutes. Keep them hot on a serving dish.

8   Drain off the butter in which the cutlets were cooked, add the shallots to the pan. After 20 seconds, deglaze with the vinegar and then with the white wine. Add the boar stock and the crushed juniper berries and reduce until you have 8 tablespoons of sauce. Whisk in the rest of the butter – 50 g (1¾ oz) – in small pieces and taste for seasoning. The sauce must not boil after this step.

Serving

9   Arrange the cutlets in the middle of a round heated dish. Surround with the fruit, with the different colours prettily interspersed, coat with the sauce and serve at once.

* If you cannot obtain wild boar, you can replace it with young pork, but it should be steeped for 24 hours in a marinade containing four fifths red wine, one fifth wine vinegar and flavoured with onion, herbs and peppercorns.

Editor's note   Fructidor is the twelfth month in the French Republican calendar.

Meat

Bouillonnade

La bouillonnade

For four people
Preparation time: 40 minutes
Cooking time: a few minutes

Ingredients 200 g (7 oz) fillet of beef
180 g (6¼ oz) veal tenderloin
180 g (6¼ oz) chicken breasts
4 white leaves of celery
a few sprigs of fresh tarragon
150 g (5¼ oz) carrots
the white part of a leek
1 medium onion
4 small fresh figs (when in season)
1 litre (1¾ pints) well-flavoured poultry stock
   (page 27)
1 teaspoon tomato purée
2 tablespoons wine vinegar
salt, freshly-ground pepper

Preparation

1 Trim the three kinds of meat and cut into medallions of 20 to 25 g ($\frac{3}{4}$ to 1 oz) each. Arrange them in the shape of a rose on a china or earthenware plate and decorate with celery leaves (the white leaves from next to the heart) and the sprigs of tarragon.

2 Peel the carrots, cut them in two lengthwise and then cut them into very fine slices on the mandoline. Remove the outer leaves from the leek without splitting it in half and cut the white part into 8 even rounds. Cut the onion into fairly thick rounds. Peel the skin from the figs, keeping them whole.

3 Take a chafing dish or, better still, a fondue dish with its own lamp. Pour in the stock, the tomato purée and the vinegar, bring to the boil and add the carrots and figs, and allow to cook for 5 minutes.

Serving

4 Bring the plate of meat to the table and put the chafing dish in the centre over a spirit lamp, which should be adjusted to ensure a steady boil. Add the onion, leek, celery and tarragon and half the meat to the dish and cook for one minute. Each guest, equipped with a spoon and fork and a heated soup plate, helps himself to a little of the broth, a piece of each kind of meat and the vegetables.

5 Add the rest of the meat and continue until all the ingredients and the broth are used up.

* The unusual feature of this dish is that it finishes cooking on the table, on a spirit lamp. Each guest cooks his own meat and helps himself to vegetables and broth, according to his own taste and appetite.

* This excellent dish will make the evening pass very happily when you have friends to dinner.

Coupe-jarret

Le coupe-jarret

For eight people
Preparation time: 3 hours
Cooking time: 4 to 5 hours

Ingredients   *Meats:*
1 shin of beef weighing 2 kg (4 lb 6 oz) altogether
2 ham hocks or salt pork hocks weighing 1·6 kg
    (3 lb 6 oz) altogether and soaked overnight if
    necessary
2 shins of veal weighing 2·5 kg (5¾ lb) altogether
4 knuckles of lamb weighing 1·2 kg (2½ lb) alto-
    gether
8 chicken drumsticks
beef bones

Vegetables:
250 g (8 oz) dried flageolet beans
250 g (8 oz) rice
200 g (7 oz) haricots verts
2 kg (4 lb 6 oz) carrots
1·7 kg (3 lb 13 oz) turnips
1·4 kg (3 lb 4 oz) tomatoes
1 kg (2¼ lb) celery
1 kg (2¼ lb) leeks

Other ingredients:
60 g (2 oz) butter
6 tablespoons wine vinegar
160 ml (¼ pint) walnut oil
4 tablespoons arachide oil
1 carrot
4 onions
a whole head of garlic
6 cloves
a handful of chervil sprigs
2 bouquets garnis containing parsley, chives and
    bayleaves

mustard
little gherkins
salt, coarse and fine, freshly-ground pepper

Accompanying Tomato Sauce (page 39), made with 1·4 kg
sauces (3 lb 4 oz) tomatoes
Sauce 'Albert Prost' (page 41)

1   Ask the butcher to trim the pieces of meat, and leave a little bone protruding at the narrow end; get him to tie them into shape and to allow an extra bit of string 50 cm (20 in) long, which you can attach to the handle of the pan and use to retrieve the meat when it is cooked.

Cooking the meat

Cooking times: beef 4 hours 35 minutes
ham 1 hour 5 minutes
veal 1 hour 5 minutes
lamb 35 minutes
chicken 25 minutes
vegetables 30 minutes

2   Half fill a very large stockpot with salted water and, when it is boiling, put in the shin of beef and fill up the spaces with the beef bones. Let it simmer for 2 hours, uncovered, and from time to time remove the fat and scum that rise to the surface with a skimmer. Then add 2 onions, cut in half and lightly browned in the oven on a baking sheet, the whole head of garlic stuck with 4 cloves and a bouquet garni. Let it bubble very gently in just one spot on the surface of the liquid for a further 1 hour 30 minutes.

3   After the beef has been cooking for 3 hours 30 minutes, take out the beef bones and replace them with the ham or salt pork and the veal. Thirty minutes later add the lamb and, 5 minutes after that, the prepared vegetables (see step 9), each variety tied up separately in a muslin bag. Wait another 5 minutes and finally add the chicken drumsticks.

4   After 25 minutes (a total of 4 hours 35 minutes since the beef went in) all the ingredients will be done. To stop them cooking any further, take the stockpot off the heat and pour in 1 litre (1¾ pints) cold water.

(continued on the next page)

Preparing the vegetables and sauces

5   Soak the dried flageolet beans in warm water for 3 hours and then put them to cook in plenty of cold water. Add a carrot, an onion stuck with 2 cloves, a bouquet garni and a handful of coarse salt. Bring to the boil and skim, then let them cook gently for up to 2 hours – the cooking time will depend on their quality.

6   Chop half the fourth onion in butter and sauté for 2 minutes. Measure the rice into a bowl and add to the onion, stir it round, then cover with boiling salted water to one and a half times the volume of the rice. Bring to the boil, cover with a sheet of greaseproof paper and the lid and cook on a medium heat for 18 minutes. Remove from the heat, let it rest for 20 minutes and fluff up the rice with a fork to separate the grains.

7   Cook the haricots verts in plenty of salted water in the usual way, for anything between 3 and 8 minutes, keeping them crisp.

8   Prepare the tomato sauce (see page 39) using 1·4 kg (3 lbs 4 oz) of tomatoes.

9   Peel and trim the carrots, turnips, celery and leeks. With a vegetable knife, cut 36 large 'cork' shapes from the carrots and 24 from the turnips, cut the celery into 24 sticks 5 cm (2 in) long and reserve just the white parts of the leeks, keeping them whole.

10   Prepare the two vinaigrette sauces. For the chicken, mix 4 tablespoons vinegar, salt and pepper and 8 tablespoons walnut oil in a bowl. At the last moment, add a good handful of chervil leaves. For the cooked flageolets, mix a tablespoon of mustard, 2 tablespoons vinegar, salt and pepper and 4 tablespoons arachide oil.

11   Make the Sauce 'Albert Prost' (page 41), for the veal.

Serving

12   Carve and serve the meat on a board in front of your guests, in the following order: first, the ham or pork, accompanied by the warm flageolet beans dressed with their vinaigrette; next, the veal, together with the rice, everything lightly coated with the Sauce 'Albert Prost'; the beef, accompanied by the turned vegetables (first removing them from their muslin bags) and served with mustard, ·

gherkins and coarse salt; then the lamb covered with the tomato sauce; and finally, the chicken drumsticks with their vinaigrette and with the haricots verts, reheated in boiling salted water, scattered over the top.

* This dish is made up of five different meats, whose common factor is that they come from the foreleg of the animal. They are boiled and served hot with different garnishes and sauces. You will need plenty of time to prepare this dish and a hearty appetite.

Editor's note   This dish was inspired by Dodin–Bouffant's dinner for the Prince of Eurasia, described in Marcel Rouff's *La vie et la passion de Dodin-Bouffant, gourmet.*

(see colour illustration opposite page 224)

Saddle of Lamb with Broad Beans

Canon d'agneau aux fèves

For four people
Preparation time: 45 minutes
Cooking time: 15 minutes

Ingredients   1 saddle of lamb weighing 2 kg (4 lb 6 oz)
1 kg (2¼ lb) fresh broad beans
70 g (2½ oz) butter
1 shallot, finely chopped
5 tablespoons dry white wine
200 ml (⅓ pint) double cream
salt, freshly-ground pepper

1 Prepare the lamb in the following way, or ask the butcher to do it for you. Carve off the two large fillets from the saddle, following the line of the bones, then turn it over and carefully cut out the two 'filets mignons' which lie underneath. Remove the sinews from the two large fillets with a sharp pointed knife, leaving a fine layer of fat on the leanest part, and take off the light skin covering the filets mignons. Season all four fillets. Using a cleaver, chop the bones of the saddle into tiny bits.

2 Heat the oven to 230° C/450° F/Mark 8. Shell the beans and skin them.

3 Heat a large wide casserole, put in 40 g ($1\frac{1}{2}$ oz) butter and, when it is hot, put in the large fillets and fill up the spaces between them with the bones. Cook in the oven for 4 minutes and then turn them over without piercing the meat. Cook for another 4 minutes and set them aside, uncovered, in a warm place. It's a good idea to put them on an upturned plate placed in a larger dish so that they don't go on cooking or soak in their own juices.

4 Drain the cooking butter into a small frying-pan, heat it and sauté the two 'filets mignons', cooking them for 2 minutes on each side. Reserve with the large fillets.

5 Drain away any remaining fat from the casserole, but leave the bones, and throw in the chopped shallot. Let it sweat for 2 minutes, then deglaze the pan with the white wine and, when this is reduced, add the cream. Cook over a gentle heat until the sauce seems to be lightly thickened, then remove it from the heat and keep it hot. Taste for seasoning.

6 Meanwhile, cook the broad beans in boiling salted water for 5 minutes, drain and then sauté in the frying-pan with 30 g (1 oz) butter. Strain the sauce through a fine wire strainer.

7 Cut the lamb fillets into 1 cm ($\frac{1}{2}$ in) slices and arrange them, over-lapping in a circle, on a heated serving dish, with the beans piled in the middle. Coat the lamb lightly with a little of the sauce and serve the rest in a sauce boat.

Shoulder of Kid with Fresh Onions

Épaule de chevreau aux oignons nouveaux

For four people
Preparation time: 30 minutes
Cooking time: 35 minutes

Ingredients
2 shoulders of kid, weighing about 900 g (2 lb) each
10 new onions, weighing about 500 g (1 lb 2 oz)
100 g (3½ oz) butter
5 tablespoons dry white wine
4 tablespoons demi-glace (page 29)
20 tarragon leaves
salt, freshly-ground pepper

Preparation

1 It is essential that the kid should be of good quality and hung for 3 to 4 days. Do not bone the shoulders but simply season with salt and pepper.

2 Choose new white onions, peel them, leave on 5 cm (2 in) of stalk, cut them in four and cut away the root base. Then separate the layers by hand – it is the way the onions are cut which gives the dish its characteristic style. Remove the stalks from the tarragon, keeping the leaves whole.

Cooking

3 Preheat the oven to 200°C/400°F/Mark 6. Heat a roasting tin large enough to hold the meat, and melt 50 g (1¾ oz) butter in it. Brown the meat in the hot butter making sure it is a good golden colour on all sides, put in the onions and place in the oven for 24 minutes.

4 Remove the roasting tin from the oven and take out the meat. Then deglaze the pan with the white wine, over a moderate heat, let it reduce until it has evaporated and then add 2 glasses of water and the meat glaze. Reduce for a further 10 minutes, ending up with 8 generous tablespoons of sauce.

5 Return the kid to the pan and simmer for a few moments, taking care not to break up the pieces of onion. Stir in the rest of the butter – 50 g (1¾ oz) – in small pieces, check the seasoning and add the whole tarragon leaves.

Serving

6 This dish must be eaten burning hot, so carve the shoulders very quickly and serve on very hot plates.

* Accompany with Mother Carles' Potatoes (page 236).

* Milk-fed lamb can be substituted for kid.

Veal with Mustard Seeds

Les corsus de veau aux graines de moutarde

For four people
Preparation time: 20 minutes
Cooking time: 2 minutes

Ingredients   500 g (1 lb 2 oz) loin of veal with all sinew and fat
removed
60 g (2 oz) white mustard seeds
3 teaspoons pale Dijon mustard
2½ tablespoons arachide oil
50 g (1¾ oz) butter
2½ tablespoons meat glaze (page 30), (optional)
1 teaspoon tarragon mustard
salt, freshly-ground pepper

1   Slice the loin of veal across the grain of the fillet into 16 little escalopes, 4 per person. Season these 'misers' lightly with salt and pepper and place them between two sheets of oiled greaseproof paper. Flatten them evenly all over with the flat side of a cleaver or steak beater so that they end up about 12 cm (5 in) long, 8 cm (3 in) across and 5 mm ($\frac{1}{4}$ in) thick. Take off the top sheet of paper and 'breadcrumb' the meat with the mustard seeds, pressing them in gently so that they stick to the surface. Put back the greaseproof paper, turn the escalopes over and, with a pastry brush, paint the other side with the pale Dijon mustard.

2   Heat the oil and 20 g ($\frac{3}{4}$ oz) butter in a tinned copper sauté pan. When a blue haze rises, put in the escalopes, seeded side down and without overlapping. Let them cook for one minute, turn them over and give them one minute on the other side. Take out the meat and keep hot on a heated dish covered with an upturned soup plate.

3   Drain the cooking fat from the pan so that you have only the brown bits sticking to the bottom (these will give body to the sauce). Deglaze the pan with 5 tablespoons water and let it reduce by two thirds. Then add the meat glaze, and reduce again until you have 5 tablespoons of sauce. If you don't have any meat glaze handy, add 2$\frac{1}{2}$ tablespoons water in the same way but don't reduce quite so much.

4   Put the meat back into the pan, together with the juice it has released, cover and keep on a low heat without boiling. This is very important, because boiling would toughen the veal.

5   One minute before serving, arrange the escalopes, slightly overlapping and with the 'seed' side uppermost, on a very hot dish. Away from the heat, dissolve the tarragon mustard in the sauce, add the rest of the butter – 30 g (1 oz) – cut into small pieces and shake the pan to melt the butter and emulsify it with the sauce. Pour the sauce on to the meat and serve with Pumpkin Fritters (page 244).

* In our local patois, 'corsus' means miser. Because the veal in this dish is served in tiny escalopes of about 35 g (1$\frac{1}{4}$ oz), we decided to use the word in our title.

Veal Chops with Watercress

Côtes de veau cressonnière

For four people
Preparation time: 40 minutes
Cooking time: 25 minutes

Ingredients   4 veal chops of 180 g (6¼ oz) each, cut from between
the second and fifth rib
60 g (2 oz) butter
300 g (10½ oz) watercress
1 shallot, finely chopped
250 ml (scant half pint) double cream
juice of ½ lemon
salt, freshly-ground pepper

1   Remove the leaves from the watercress one by one, wash and drain them and set 24 of the leaves aside.

2   Take a tinned copper sauté pan or, failing that, a frying-pan, of the right size so that the four chops fit neatly beside each other without any spaces in between. Heat it, put in the butter and, when it is a hazelnut brown, put in the chops seasoned with salt and pepper. Cook for 15 to 20 minutes altogether so that they are nicely coloured on both sides. Take out the meat and keep warm in a heated dish.

3   Soften the chopped shallot for 2 minutes in the cooking butter without browning, deglaze the pan with 2 to 3 tablespoons of water and add the watercress and the cream. Bring to the boil and seal the pan tightly, using an upturned lid filled with ice cubes, so that the steam forming inside will condense and drop back into the sauce.

4   After 12 minutes, take off the lid, taste for seasoning and add a few drops of lemon juice. Return the chops to the sauce and allow to simmer very gently for 3 minutes.

5   Arrange the meat on a serving plate on top of the watercress sauce and decorate with the 24 watercress leaves which you set aside earlier.

* To accompany, serve rice cooked as for Coupe-jarret (page 188).

Veal Kidneys with White Haricot Beans

Emincé de rognons de veau aux haricots blancs

For four people
Preparation time: 30 minutes
Cooking time: 12 minutes

Ingredients 1 kg (2¼ lb) veal kidneys (4 kidneys)
500 g (1 lb 2 oz) fresh white haricot beans in their
   shells or 400 g (14 oz) dried white haricot beans
   (see note)
1 carrot
1 onion stuck with 2 cloves
a bouquet garni
coarse salt
25 g (1 oz) butter
1 shallot, chopped
150 ml (¼ pint) red wine (for instance, Beaujolais
   Villages)
5 tablespoons demi-glace (page 29)
400 ml (¾ pint) double cream
1 teaspoon Dijon mustard
2–3 sprigs of parsley, coarsely chopped
salt, freshly-ground pepper

Editor's note   Certain varieties of French beans are grown past the 'haricots verts' stage and allowed to develop full-sized haricot beans, which are ready to eat towards the end of the summer. They are picked and sold in their shells, and then provide a rather long-winded job, since shelling them is not easy. However, they are worth the trouble since they are much creamier and more delicate than dried beans. They are cooked as they are, without soaking. If you can't obtain or grow fresh haricot beans, dried beans can be substituted but will need soaking.

One or two hours in advance

1 Shell the white beans and put them in a pan in plenty of cold water. Add the carrot, the onion stuck with cloves, the bouquet garni and a handful of coarse salt. Bring to the boil, skim and cook gently for about 1 hour, depending on their quality. (Dried beans will take up to 2 hours.)

2 Remove the casing of fat round the kidneys without damaging the tight transparent membrane which covers them. Make a lengthwise incision in the kidneys and extract the largest of the veins and nerves from the centre.

Cooking

3 Preheat the oven to 220° C/425° F/Mark 7. Heat the butter in a fireproof dish, put in the kidneys, seasoned with salt and pepper, side by side and seize them on all sides. When they are nicely browned, cook in the oven for 12 minutes.

4 Take out the kidneys and soften the shallot in the same butter for 1 minute. Deglaze with the red wine, add the demi-glace, bring to the boil and allow to reduce by half. Add the cream and bring back to the boil. You should have a very light sauce.

5 Wipe the kidneys with a cloth to remove any surplus fat and then slice them on a board into slices 1 cm ($\frac{1}{2}$ in) thick.

6 Dissolve the mustard in a bowl with a little of the sauce and then incorporate the mixture into the sauce, together with the kidneys, the cooked beans, well drained, and the parsley. Allow to simmer over a gentle heat for 2 to 3 minutes without boiling, which would toughen the kidneys. Serve at once.

Veal with Leeks

Sauté de veau aux poireaux

For four people
Preparation time: 30 minutes
Cooking time: 1 hour 15 minutes

Ingredients 800 g (1 lb 12 oz) shin of veal, cut from the upper
part of the leg
800 g (1 lb 12 oz) white parts of leek
40 g (1½ oz) sultanas
40 g (1½ oz) butter
5 tablespoons arachide oil
5 tablespoons dry white wine
a bouquet garni
200 ml (⅓ pint) milk
juice of ½ lemon
salt, freshly-ground pepper

1   Cut the veal into pieces weighing about 40 g (1½ oz), keeping the individual muscles whole as far as possible, and season with salt and pepper. Slice the leeks evenly. Soak the sultanas in cold water.

2   Heat the butter and the oil in a heavy copper saucepan or a casserole, large enough to hold all the pieces of meat side by side. Put in the pieces of veal and allow them to brown for about 15 minutes, turning them around carefully without piercing them. Turn down the heat and add the leeks, cover the pan and let them sweat for 10 minutes without browning. Add the white wine and the bouquet garni, pour on the milk and cook for just under 30 minutes. The sauce will thicken of its own accord.

3   Make sure that the veal is tender, remove the bouquet garni and add the drained sultanas and a few drops of the lemon juice. Taste for seasoning and serve.

Breast of Veal with Salsify

Tendrons de veau braisés aux salsifis

For four people
Preparation time: 40 minutes
Cooking time: approximately 2 hours

Ingredients   4 breasts of veal, weighing 300 g (10½ oz) each (see
        note)
    flour
    1 kg (2¼ lb) salsify
    20 button onions
    150 g (5¼ oz) lean green streaky bacon
    50 g (1¾ oz) butter
    1 litre (1¾ pints) poultry stock (page 27)
    a bouquet garni
    a few sprigs of chervil and parsley, coarsely
        chopped
    salt, freshly-ground pepper

Editor's note   Tendron is the cut of veal most often used for stewing
in France – it is the part of the breast which contains the cartilaginous
false ribs and is very gelatinous. If you can't obtain this cut, use
knuckle which is also gelatinous.

Preparation

1 Peel the salsify with a potato peeler, cut into 5 cm (2 in) lengths and reserve in a bowl of water acidulated with a few drops of vinegar. Peel the onions.

2 Cut the bacon into lardons 1 cm ($\frac{1}{2}$ in) thick and 4 cm (1$\frac{1}{2}$ in) long. Blanch them in boiling water, refresh in cold water and drain.

Cooking

3 Take a heavy casserole, preferably enamelled cast iron, large enough to take the breasts side by side without overlapping. Melt the butter in the casserole and throw in the lardons and, when they are nicely browned, take them out with a slotted spoon. Repeat the operation with the onions, frying them to a golden brown in the bacon fat, and set them aside with the lardons.

4 Season the breasts of veal with salt and pepper, dust them with flour, put them in the casserole, side by side, and let them brown over a moderate heat for at least 20 minutes. Then take them out and put them on one side with the lardons and onions.

5 Preheat the oven to 150° C/300° F/Mark 2. Dry and season the salsify, put in the same casserole and fry them gently for about 20 minutes. Put back the veal and the bacon and onions, pour on the stock, add the bouquet garni, bring to the boil and seal the pan hermetically. Let it simmer steadily in the oven for 1 hour 15 minutes. The liquid should reduce by about half, becoming syrupy and an appetising brown.

Finishing and serving

6 Take the casserole out of the oven and let it rest away from the heat for a few moments so that the fat can rise to the surface. Skim off the fat with a spoon and remove the bouquet garni. Add the chervil and parsley and taste for seasoning.

7 Arrange the breasts of veal, overlapping, on a large heated serving dish and cover with the salsify and the cooking juices.

Raw Beef with Digoinaise Sauce

Boeuf cru sauce Digoinaise

For four people
Preparation time: 30 minutes

Ingredients   560 g (1¼ lb) best entrecôte steak
80 watercress leaves
salt
Digoinaise Sauce (page 42)

1   Prepare the Digoinaise sauce.

2   Ask for a piece of beef close to the first rib, which has less waste, and make sure that the meat has been well hung, for at least 15 days, and that the flesh is generously marbled with fat. Cut into very fine slices with a ham knife or bacon slicer.

3   Take the leaves of watercress off the stalks, wash them in plenty of cold water and drain.

4   Take four large chilled plates or individual dishes, cover them completely with the slices of beef and sprinkle lightly with salt. Using a tablespoon, pour the sauce in a ring round the meat and decorate with the watercress leaves to heighten the colour of the meat. Eat with brown bread, not too fresh.

Calf's Head with Marrow

Tête de veau amourette

For four people
Preparation time: 2 hours
Cooking time: 2 hours

Ingredients
500 g (1 lb 2 oz) calf's head, boned and prepared
   by the butcher
100 g (3½ oz) veal tongue
100 g (3½ oz) spinal marrow – this is the long white
   nerve from the spine of a veal calf
150 g (5¼ oz) potatoes
24 green olives
5 tomatoes
1 carrot
1 onion
2½ tablespoons olive oil
2½ tablespoons cognac
5 tablespoons dry white wine
300 ml (½ pint) demi-glace (page 29)
a bouquet garni
flour
20 g (¾ oz) butter
1 tablespoon wine vinegar
fresh parsley, chopped
salt, freshly-ground pepper

Editor's note   *Amourettes.* The white strip of nerves found in the
spinal column of veal calves (and of lambs) is considered a delicacy
in both France and Italy. It has a brain-like texture, but is a little
firmer and less likely to fall apart in cooking. The flavour too
resembles that of brains, so if you cannot obtain amourettes, substitute calves' brains, removing blood and nerves carefully after soaking
and before blanching.
You may have to buy a whole prepared calf's head to make this
dish, in which case it must be boned – ask the butcher to do this
for you and to set aside the tongue (to be used in the dish) and the
brains (if you are using them instead of the amourettes).

1   Blanch the calf's head and the tongue by putting in cold water and bringing to the boil for 3 to 4 minutes, refresh in cold water, skin the tongue and cut the head and tongue into pieces of about 20 g ($\frac{3}{4}$ oz). Soak the spinal marrow in cold water for 1 hour and then blanch for a minute in boiling salted water with a few drops of vinegar.

2   Cut the potatoes into four and then 'turn' them into large cork shapes. Stone the olives and blanch them in boiling water for 2–3 minutes. Skin the tomatoes, halve them, press out excess moisture and pips in the palm of your hand and chop them coarsely. Cut the carrot and the onion into mirepoix dice.

3   Put the oil in a casserole, heat it and cook the pieces of head and tongue for 25 minutes. Stir all the time with a wooden spatula to stir up the thin glaze which forms on the bottom of the pan.

4   Add the carrot and onion and sweat for 5 minutes, deglaze with the cognac and then the white wine and finally pour on the demi-glace. Put in the bouquet garni, cover the pan and cook for 1 hour. Add the potatoes and cook for a further 30 minutes.

5   Cut the spinal marrow into pieces 5 cm (2 in) long, roll them in flour and fry them to a golden brown in a frying-pan. Deglaze the pan with the vinegar.

6   Add the spinal marrow and the olives to the casserole and check the seasoning, adding a generous amount of pepper. Let it simmer for 10 minutes and finish with a good handful of very fresh, coarsely chopped parsley. Serve very hot.

Beef 'Fleurie'

Côte de boeuf au Fleurie

For four people
Preparation time: 30 minutes
Cooking time: 30 minutes

Ingredients 120 g (5 oz) beef marrow
1 piece of rib of beef weighing 1·3 kg (2 lb 12 oz)
180 g (6¼ oz) butter
2 grey shallots, finely chopped
250 ml (scant half pint) red Burgundy, preferably
  Fleurie
4 tablespoons of meat glaze (page 30)
salt, freshly-ground pepper

One day in advance

1 Buy the marrow bones the day before and have them sawn up. Remove the marrow and soak it for 12 hours in cold water.

2 Get the butcher to cut a piece of beef taken from between the second and third rib and ask him to trim the bone to make a sort of handle such as you have on a lamb cutlet.

Preparing and cooking

3 Season the beef with salt and pepper. In a tinned copper sauté pan, heat 40 g (1½ oz) butter to a hazelnut brown, put in the meat and cook for about 15 minutes on each side, basting frequently with a spoon. Put the beef on one side on an upturned plate inside a dish, so that it doesn't sit in its own juices, and let it rest in a warm place for at least 20 minutes – which is about the time it takes to complete the sauce.

4 Meanwhile, poach the marrow as follows. Cut the marrow into pieces 1 cm (½ in) thick, put them into a small saucepan and cover with cold salted water. Heat through slowly and when the water reaches boiling point take the pan off the heat.

5 Transfer the cooking butter from the sauté pan to a frying-pan. Put the shallot into the sauté pan (without butter) and let it soften gently. Deglaze with the red wine, add the meat glaze and let it reduce by a good half. Take the pan off the heat and gradually whisk in the rest of the butter – 140 g (4¾ oz) – in small pieces. At this stage, the sauce must not boil again and should be kept at a temperature of 70° C/185° F. If it does get any hotter than this, the sauce will separate and you will have to use cold water to recover it. Taste for seasoning and strain through a fine conical strainer.

Finishing and serving

6 Reheat the beef in the frying-pan with the cooking butter, then arrange it on a heated serving dish. Add the juice, which has seeped out of the meat while it was resting, to the sauce, then pour it lightly over the beef. Drain the marrow and arrange it carefully on top of the beef. Carve the beef into 8 slices parallel to the bone and serve it with Forézienne Potatoes (page 234).

'Ten plus Ten' Steak

Entrecôte dix sur dix

For four people
Preparation time: 30 minutes
Cooking time: 30 minutes for the sauce,
  20 seconds for the entrecôtes

Ingredients

1·2 kg (1 lb 9 oz) beef entrecôte in one piece
70 g (2½ oz) butter
2 medium onions, chopped
4 tablespoons wine vinegar
5 tablespoons red wine, preferably Beaujolais
  Villages
½ tablespoon tomato purée
a sprig of thyme
2 tablespoons arachide oil
parsley, ⎱
chervil, ⎰ separated into tiny sprigs
tarragon leaves
salt, coarse and fine, black peppercorns

1 Have the beef cut from between the third and fourth ribs and cut it into 12 very thin entrecôtes – or ask the butcher to do it for you. Each one should weigh about 75 g (2½ oz) after trimming. Season the entrecôtes lightly.

2 Heat 20 g (¾ oz) butter in a sauté pan and soften the onions for 5 minutes, without letting them brown and stirring with a wooden spoon. Deglaze the pan with the vinegar and let it evaporate completely. Then add the red wine, half a teaspoon coarsely crushed peppercorns, the tomato purée, the thyme and a little coarse salt, and simmer very gently for 20 minutes. You should end up with about 3 tablespoons of sauce. Take out the thyme and gradually incorporate 30 g (1 oz) butter, cut in small pieces, whisking vigorously. Taste for seasoning and keep the sauce hot, taking care not to let it boil.

3 Heat 20 g (¾ oz) butter and the oil in a very large frying-pan. (The addition of the oil means that you can seize the meat at a higher temperature.) As soon as the butter and oil begin to smoke, fry the meat for 10 seconds on each side, turning it over without piercing it. Depending on the size of your pan, you may have to cook the meat in several batches; the cooked steaks can be kept hot on an upturned plate placed in a heated baking tin. But try to complete the whole operation as quickly as possible so that the steaks, which are very thin, do not spoil.

4 Take four large very hot plates and arrange 3 entrecôtes on each, without overlapping. Spread the hot sauce on top with the back of a spoon and sprinkle with the parsley, chervil and tarragon leaves. Serve immediately, accompanied by Gaufrette Potatoes (page 235).

Editor's note The 'dix sur dix' of the title refers to the cooking time – ten seconds on each side is all that's needed for these very thinly cut entrecôtes.

Fillets of Beef with Shallots

Filet mignon de boeuf aux échalotes

For four people
Preparation time: 20 minutes
Cooking time: 5 minutes

Ingredients

840 g (1 lb 14 oz) trimmed fillet of beef
60 g (2 oz) butter
$2\frac{1}{2}$ tablespoons wine vinegar
200 ml (scant half pint) tomato-flavoured demi-
     glace (page 29)
5 tablespoons double cream
80 g ($2\frac{3}{4}$ oz) shallots
salt, freshly-ground pepper

1   Make sure that the fillet is completely trimmed of fat and sinew and cut it into 24 pieces about 2 cm ($\frac{3}{4}$ in) thick and weighing 35 g ($1\frac{1}{4}$ oz) each.

2   Take a heavy frying-pan, large enough to hold the fillets side by side in one layer, and heat 25 g (1 oz) butter until foaming. Season the steaks lightly with salt and pepper and sear them for 2 minutes on each side. Take them out and reserve on a heated plate placed upside down in a dish so that they don't sit in their own juices.

3   Pour off the cooking butter (which can be used on the accompanying vegetables), deglaze the pan with the vinegar and let it evaporate completely. Then add the demi-glace and the cream and let it simmer gently until it has reduced to about 8 tablespoons of sauce. Add the juices which have run out of the steaks, remove from the heat and whisk in the rest of the butter, cut into small pieces. Taste for seasoning. Put the fillets back into the sauce and simmer very gently for 20 seconds without boiling.

4   Arrange the fillets on a very hot serving dish, coat them lightly with the sauce and sprinkle with the raw shallots, coarsely chopped at the last minute to keep their freshness.

* Serve with wood mushrooms (millers) or other wild mushrooms according to the season.

Pork Chops with Confucius Sauce

Côtelettes de porc sauce confuse

For four people
Preparation time: 20 minutes
Cooking time: 40 minutes

Ingredients

4 pork chops, trimmed, weighing 180 g (6¼ oz)
    each or 720 g (1 lb 9 oz) altogether
1 orange
1 tomato
4 cloves of garlic
1 large onion
40 g (1½ oz) butter
juice of ½ lemon
4 fresh mint leaves
300 ml (½ pint) demi-glace (page 29)
salt, freshly-ground pepper

Editor's note   The sauce in this dish was created more or less hapha-
zardly, hence its name 'confuse'. However, on a trip by leading French
chefs to China in 1978, the sauce aroused great interest among
the Chinese who mistakenly assumed it had something to do with
Confucius.

1 If possible, ask the butcher to trim the chops, shortening the bone and removing the chine bone and excess fat. Season them with salt and pepper.

2 Peel the orange, removing every trace of skin and pith, slice into rounds and take out the pips. Slice the tomato and remove the seeds. Choose small garlic cloves, peel them, cut them in half lengthwise and blanch for 5 minutes in boiling salted water. Chop the onion coarsely.

3 Heat half the butter – 20 g ($\frac{3}{4}$ oz) – in a sauté pan and put in the chops side by side. Sear them for 5 to 6 minutes, turn them over and sear the other side for a further 5 to 6 minutes, then lower the heat and finish cooking them gently for about 15 minutes, turning them over from time to time. When they are cooked, keep them hot in a serving dish.

4 Brown the onion and the garlic in the cooking fat until they are a dark brown, stirring all the time. Cover the pan with a saucepan lid and tilt it, straining off the fat into a bowl, but leaving the vegetables in the pan. Deglaze the pan with the lemon juice, add the mint and the sliced tomato and orange, pour on the demi-glace and bring to the boil. Reduce until you have the right amount of sauce for the chops, about 200 ml ($\frac{1}{3}$ pint). Taste for seasoning and whisk in the rest of the butter – 20 g ($\frac{3}{4}$ oz) – cut in small pieces.

5 Arrange the chops on a serving dish, cover with the orange and tomato slices and coat with the sauce.

Blade Steak of Pork

Palette de porc 'pauvre femme'

For four people
Preparation time: 50 minutes
Cooking time: 1 hour 30 minutes

Ingredients   900 g (2 lb) blade of pork on the bone
3 cloves of garlic
800 g (1 lb 12 oz) onions, finely chopped
100 g (3½ oz) butter
1 potato, peeled and cut into rounds
a bouquet garni
250 ml (scant half pint) milk
a sprig of flat parsley
salt, freshly-ground pepper

1 Choose a piece of pork with the palest pink flesh. Peel the garlic, cut the cloves lengthwise in two and insert them into six small incisions made in the meat. Season with salt and pepper.

2 Melt 20 g (¾ oz) butter in a heavy casserole and brown the meat lightly on both sides for 15 minutes. At the same time, fry the onions in a frying-pan with the rest of the butter – 80 g (2¾ oz) – until they are a nice golden colour. Add the onions to the pork, together with the sliced potato and the bouquet garni. Bring the milk to the boil and pour it over the meat. Cover the pan and cook for 1 hour 15 minutes on a low heat, turning the meat from time to time.

3 Take out the meat and keep it hot on a fireproof dish. Remove the bouquet garni and purée the onions and potato through the mouli-légumes, together with the cooking liquid, making a light purée. Skim off any excess fat which rises to the surface of the purée and taste for seasoning, adding a generous quantity of pepper. Pour the purée over the meat and let it simmer for a few moments.

4 Sprinkle with parsley leaves and serve in the dish. It can be accompanied with Green Cabbage with Bacon (page 226).

Roanne Ham with Ribbon Vegetables

Jambon de Roanne enrubanné

For four people
Preparation time: 45 minutes
Cooking time: 10 minutes

Ingredients 4 slices, weighing 120 g (4½ oz) each, of Roanne ham
4 vegetable spirals (see page 249)
140 g (5 oz) butter
juice of ½ lemon
salt, freshly-ground pepper

---

1 First prepare the vegetable spirals, (see steps 1 and 2 on page 249).

2 Sauté the slices of ham in a frying-pan with 20 g (¾ oz) butter until golden on both sides and then arrange on a serving dish.

3 Heat 2½ tablespoons water in a small pan and, over a high heat, whisk in the butter cut in small pieces until completely emulsified. Add salt and pepper and a few drops of lemon juice.

4 Place the slices of ham on four heated plates and decorate with the vegetable coils in the centre. Unroll them slightly at the edges and spread them out so that they cover the whole plate nicely; coat lightly with the butter sauce.

* Roanne ham is cured in straw and stuck with green peppercorns. The recipe will work with York ham or unsmoked ham.

Vegetables

Cooking Green Vegetables

Cuisson des légumes verts

Here we give you the basic rules for the successful cooking of French beans, peas, spinach, asparagus tips, etc. You probably need no reminder that they should remain slightly crisp under the teeth and that prolonged cooking ruins their flavour, texture and colour.

1   Use a copper saucepan, preferably untinned, or failing this, a stainless steel pan.

2   Plunge the vegetables into a generous quantity of boiling water, salted with 10 g ($\frac{1}{4}$ oz) salt per litre ($1\frac{3}{4}$ pints).

3   Never cover the pan.

4   Keep the water boiling rapidly throughout the cooking time.

5   Drain the vegetables the moment that they are cooked, give them their appropriate seasoning and serve them at once.

If the vegetables do have to wait, as so often happens, they should be refreshed rapidly in cold water as soon as they are cooked, or even better, have ready a bowl of cold water with a few ice cubes floating in it and transfer the vegetables straight from the pan to the bowl with a slotted spoon. When they have cooled, drain them and keep in a cool place until they are needed.

To serve the vegetables 'à l'anglaise', plunge them back into boiling water just long enough to heat them right through without cooking, drain, season and serve.

Cooking Asparagus

Cuisson des asperges

Although cooking asparagus is simplicity itself, there are three important rules.

1 Choose freshly cut asparagus. You can tell how fresh it is by looking at the cut ends.

2 You should peel them with a swivelling potato peeler. When you are sure that they are properly peeled, remove any small loose leaves around the heads, wash them and tie them together in bundles of 8 or 10 spears. Trim them to an equal length of 18 cm (7 in).

3 Overcooked asparagus loses its flavour. We advise cooking it for about 13 to 18 minutes, according to how thick it is.

Cook in the usual way, by plunging the bundles into boiling salted water, but don't refresh them.

* Allow a little under 490 g (about 1 lb) asparagus per person.

Aubergines Stendhal

Aubergines Stendhal

For four people
Preparation time: 30 minutes
Cooking time: 30 minutes

Ingredients   4 long aubergines, weighing 150 g (5¼ oz) each
400 g (14 oz) tomatoes
200 g (7 oz) butter
a whole head of garlic
4 leaves of fresh basil
salt, freshly-ground pepper

1   Choose good aubergines all of the same size and shape, very fresh, glossy and a deep violet colour. Wipe them clean, cut off the ends and then, with a long knife, make four deep lengthwise cuts in each. Put them on a dish and sprinkle lightly with salt and freshly-ground pepper. Leave for about 15 minutes.

2   Cut the tomatoes in half. Slice them 1 cm ($\frac{1}{2}$ in) thick, to give about 32 half slices. Season them and then insert two slices side by side right into each of the cuts in the aubergines. Tie up the aubergines with string, fairly tightly, to hold them in their original shape and enclose the tomatoes.

3   Arrange the aubergines in a saucepan just large enough to take them in one layer. Add the butter, the whole head of garlic and 750 ml ($1\frac{1}{4}$ pints) salted water. Cover the pan and cook on a low heat for 30 minutes.

4   Take out the aubergines with a large fork and put them on a flameproof gratin dish. Reduce the cooking liquid until you have about 8 tablespoons of syrupy juice. Take the strings off the aubergines, pour the sauce over them, and simmer for a few moments. Sprinkle with freshly chopped basil and serve very hot.

* For a cold variation of this dish, replace the butter with 200 ml ($\frac{1}{3}$ pint) olive oil and add the juice of half a lemon and a bouquet garni. Let it reduce for longer, until you have only 6 tablespoons of sauce, and keep in a cool place overnight. Serve the following day, at room temperature.

Editor's note   The Stendhal of the title is an allusion to the connection between *Le rouge et le noir* and the appearance of this dish.

Swiss Chard with Blue Cheese

Côtes de blettes à la Fourme de Montbrison

For four people
Preparation time: 30 minutes
Cooking time: 30 minutes

Ingredients

900 g (2 lb) Swiss chard
2 egg yolks
300 ml ($\frac{1}{2}$ pint) double cream
50 g ($1\frac{3}{4}$ oz) butter
80 g ($2\frac{3}{4}$ oz) Montbrison cheese (see note)
salt, freshly-ground pepper

1 Strip the green leaves from the chard stalks so that you are left with only the white ribs. Pull away any strings and strip off the thin skin covering them, then cut them into strips 4 cm ($1\frac{1}{2}$ in) by 2 cm ($\frac{3}{4}$ in). Wash and drain them.

2 Mix two egg yolks in a bowl with 1 tablespoon cream.

3 Heat the butter in a casserole, add the chard, cover the pan and cook gently for 15 minutes. Then add the rest of the cream and finish cooking for about 10 minutes over a very low heat.

4 Melt the cheese over a gentle flame in a separate small saucepan and, when it is softened to a thick cream, add it to the chard. Away from the heat, incorporate the egg and cream liaison and mix it in without letting it boil. Taste for seasoning, adding salt and pepper if necessary.

5 Transfer to a gratin dish, put quickly under the grill until the surface is a good golden colour. Serve at once.

Editor's note Similar to Fourme d'Ambert, Montbrison is a blue, cow's milk cheese, very strong in flavour and slightly bitter – you could use Gorgonzola as a substitute.

Artichokes with Chervil

Émincé d'artichaut au cerfeuil

For four people
Preparation time: 30 minutes
Cooking time: 30 minutes

Ingredients   6 medium globe artichokes
1 lemon
5 tablespoons distilled vinegar
1 shallot, chopped
30 g (1 oz) butter
2 tablespoons dry white wine
150 ml ($\frac{1}{4}$ pint) double cream
$\frac{1}{2}$ tablespoon Dijon mustard
several sprigs of fresh chervil
salt, pepper

---

1   Choose very fresh artichokes, preferably the purple ones. Break off the stalk level with the base and pull off the two rows of coarse leaves around it. With a very sharp vegetable knife, trim away the leaves to expose the bases of the artichokes, rub each one with half the lemon as soon as it is ready, and throw it straight into a bowl of cold water acidulated with 5 tablespoons vinegar to prevent it turning black. Then cut the bases into four, remove the chokes and leave in the acidulated water.

2   In a tinned copper pan, or one with a thick bottom, soften the chopped shallot in the butter without browning. Deglaze the pan with the white wine, drain the quartered artichoke bottoms and put them in. Pour in enough water to come half way up the artichokes, season with salt and pepper, seal the pan tightly and cook for 15 minutes.

3   Take off the lid and let the liquid reduce until you have about 2 tablespoons left. Add the cream, bring to the boil and simmer for a few minutes. Mix the mustard into the sauce and taste for seasoning. Serve in a deep dish, liberally sprinkled with sprigs of fresh chervil.

Green Cabbage with Bacon

Chou vert aux lardons

For four people
Preparation time: 30 minutes
Cooking time: 30 minutes

Ingredients   1 green cabbage weighing about 1 kg (2¼ lb)
120 g (4½ oz) lean streaky bacon
1 tablespoon arachide oil
80 g (2¾ oz) butter
3 tablespoons wine vinegar
salt, freshly-ground pepper

1   Choose a green cabbage or, out of season, a savoy. Separate all the leaves, discard most of the stalks and wash thoroughly. Blanch in boiling salted water for 10 minutes, refresh in cold water, drain and turn out onto the working surface. Cut the leaves across in both directions with a large knife, so that they are very coarsely chopped.

2   Cut the bacon into pieces 1 cm ($\frac{1}{2}$ in) by 5 cm (2 in), throw them into boiling water for 2 to 3 minutes and drain.

3   Preheat the oven to 190°C/375°F/Mark 5. Put the lardons into a casserole with the arachide oil, place them over a fairly brisk heat and let them brown in their own fat. Drain and keep them on one side on a dish. Put the cabbage into the pan, add 5 tablespoons water, the butter and a little salt, remembering that the bacon is already salty. Cover with a round of oiled greaseproof paper, placed directly on top of the cabbage. Cover the casserole and cook in the oven for 20 minutes.

4   Take off the lid and the paper and make sure that there is very little liquid left in the pan. Bring the vinegar to the boil in a small frying-pan and pour it over the cabbage. Add the lardons, let it simmer for 5 minutes and serve in a hot serving dish with a good twist of the peppermill.

White Beans with Red Wine

Haricots blancs au vin rouge

For four people
Preparation time: 40 minutes
Cooking time: 50 minutes

Ingredients 750 g (1 lb 10 oz) fresh white haricot beans (see
note on page 200)
1 medium onion
1 clove
$\frac{1}{2}$ carrot
a small bouquet garni
3 shallots
80 g (2$\frac{3}{4}$ oz) butter
200 ml ($\frac{1}{3}$ pint) red wine
$\frac{1}{2}$ clove of garlic
parsley
salt, freshly-ground pepper

1   Shell the beans at the last minute. Plunge them into a large sauce-pan of boiling water, salted with 7 g ($\frac{1}{4}$ oz) salt per litre (1$\frac{3}{4}$ pints) water, and skim. Add the onion stuck with a clove, the carrot and the bouquet garni and cook for 30 minutes.

2   Chop the shallots and soften them in a casserole with 40 g (1$\frac{1}{2}$ oz) butter, add the red wine and let it evaporate completely. Drain the beans of most of their liquid, keeping the rest on one side in case it is needed later, add them to the pan with the freshly chopped garlic and simmer for 10 minutes. Taste for seasoning.

3   Add the remaining butter – 40 g (1$\frac{1}{2}$ oz) – cut into pieces the size of a hazelnut and shake the casserole to make sure that the butter amalgamates evenly. The beans should now be bathed in light sauce; if this is not the case, add a few spoonfuls of their cooking liquid. Sprinkle with chopped parsley and serve.

* This dish takes kindly to being reheated.

* You can use dried white haricot beans, but you will then have to soak them in warm water for at least 2 hours and cook them for much longer.

Stuffed Lettuces

Laitues farcies à la bourbonnaise

For four people
Preparation time: 1 hour 30 minutes
Cooking time: 1 hour

Ingredients 4 lettuces with good hearts
150 g (5¼ oz) white homemade type bread, crusts
   removed
150 ml (¼ pint) whipping cream
2 poached chicken breasts
20 chives
a sprig of parsley
5 egg yolks
½ carrot
1 onion
50 g (1¾ oz) butter
2½ tablespoons dry white wine
500 ml (scant pint) poultry stock (page 27)
a bouquet garni
a piece of pork rind
salt, freshly-ground pepper

1   Choose round cabbage lettuces, trim the base to a point to stop the leaves coming off and discard any wilted leaves. Wash the lettuces carefully, blanch for 5 minutes in plenty of boiling salted water and refresh by plunging them into a bowl of cold water. Shake them in the water, head down, to remove the grit that inevitably remains, then press between your hands and leave on a rack to drain.

2   Break the bread into bits and put them in a bowl with the cream. Remove the skin from the chicken breasts, chop the meat together with the chives and parsley and add to the bowl. Work everything together vigorously with a wooden spatula, incorporating the 5 egg yolks to obtain a smooth farce.

3   Put the 4 lettuces on the worktop, divide them in half lengthwise without cutting through the base and open them up. Stuff with the farce, if necessary removing part of the heart to make room for the stuffing, then fold the leaves over it to reshape the lettuces and tie them into shape with a piece of string.

4   Cut the carrot and the onion into rounds. Heat 10 g ($\frac{1}{3}$ oz) butter in the bottom of a casserole and sweat them over a gentle heat for 5 minutes. Put the stuffed lettuces on top, deglaze the pan with the white wine, pour in the poultry stock, add the bouquet garni and salt and cover with the piece of pork rind. Bring to the boil, cover the pan and cook for about 1 hour.

5   Take out the lettuces, untie them and keep hot on a buttered dish. Remove the carrot and onion from the pan and reduce the liquid to 6 tablespoons. Then add the rest of the butter in small pieces and whisk in over a high heat. Return the lettuces to the pan and simmer for 2 to 3 minutes in their sauce.

6   Arrange the lettuces in a serving dish, coat with the sauce and serve very hot.

Curly Cucumbers in Cream

Frisons de concombres

For four people
Preparation time: 25 minutes
Cooking time: 10 minutes

Ingredients 2 cucumbers, weighing 600 g (1 lb 5 oz) altogether
200 ml ($\frac{1}{3}$ pint) double cream
juice of $\frac{1}{2}$ lemon
salt, freshly-ground pepper

Twelve hours in advance

1   Choose two very fresh cucumbers. Cut off the two ends and divide each into 4 pieces 7 to 8 cm (about 3 in) long. Peel them and with a very sharp fine-bladed knife, cut lengthwise into very thin, even slices about 2–3 mm ($\frac{1}{8}$ inch) thick at the most, and then into julienne strips. Discard the pips. Wash the cucumber julienne in a bowl of cold water and leave them to soak for 12 hours, to firm them, changing the water two or three times.

Cooking

2   Pour the cream into a medium saucepan, add salt, bring to the boil and let it reduce. Drain the cucumber strips and dry them in a cloth, then add to the cream. The liquid from the cucumbers will thin the cream, so let it boil again for 5 minutes to thicken lightly as before. Season with salt, pepper and the lemon juice.

Serving

3   Serve separately in small dishes, with fish, veal or chicken.

Steamed Potatoes and Truffles

Duo de truffes à la vapeur

For four people
Preparation time: 25 minutes
Cooking time: 25 minutes

Ingredients   160 g (6 oz) raw truffles
250 g (8¾ oz) potatoes
fresh unsalted butter
salt, coarse and fine, pepper

* A potato steamer or a saucepan with a rack that fits inside it is essential for this recipe.

1   Make sure that the truffles are very clean and brush them under running water if they are not. Cut the potatoes into the same number of pieces as there are truffles, and carve them into the same shape.

2   Fill the pan with water to the level of the rack. Lightly season the truffles and potatoes with salt and pepper and place them on the rack. Cover the pan and bring to the boil, then turn down the heat and let it simmer for 25 minutes.

3   Serving straight from the pan, cut the potatoes and truffles into two or three slices and divide them between four hot plates. Scatter a few grains of coarse salt over the top and put the butter in the middle of the table so that your guests can help themselves.

* For those who would rather do without the potatoes, it is a good idea to use a mixture of half Sauternes and half dry white wine for the cooking liquid. This enhances the scent of the truffles. You can then whisk in the butter and serve this cooking liquid as a sauce.

Forézienne Potatoes

Gratin de pommes de terre à la Forézienne

For four people
Preparation time: 20 minutes
Cooking time: 30 minutes to 1 hour

Ingredients 800 g (1 lb 12 oz) waxy potatoes, such as Pink Fir
 Apple
250 ml (scant half pint) milk
300 ml ($\frac{1}{2}$ pint) double cream
salt, freshly-ground pepper

1 Peel the long potatoes at the last minute. Slice into paper thin rounds 3 mm ($\frac{1}{8}$ in) thick and about 5 cm (2 in) in diameter. Wipe with a cloth or kitchen paper, put into a dish and season with salt and pepper.

2 Bring the milk to the boil in a deep heavy saucepan. Put the potatoes in, one round at a time, and bring back to the boil. Cover the pan and cook over a gentle heat for 5–10 minutes. When the potatoes have absorbed the milk at the end of this time, add the cream, bring to the boil again, cover and cook over a low heat until tender.

3 With a slotted spoon, transfer the potatoes to a long gratin dish. Ten to fifteen minutes before serving, put them under the grill to turn the top a lovely golden colour.

Editor's note Potatoes vary so much from variety to variety that you will have to experiment to find the right cooking time.

Gaufrette Potatoes

Pommes gaufrettes au beurre

For four people
Preparation time: 15 minutes
Cooking time: 20 minutes

Ingredients   800 g (1 lb 12 oz) waxy potatoes, making about
600 g (1 lb 5 oz) when peeled
160 g (6 oz) butter
a good pinch of salt
generous pinch of freshly-ground pepper

One day in advance

1   Peel the potatoes and cut into the shape of large corks, paring the sides and cutting off the two ends. With a mandoline cut them into gaufrettes (see note) over a bowl of cold water and soak for 12 hours, changing the water from time to time to remove all trace of starch.

Cooking

2   Preheat the oven to 230° C/450° F/Mark 8. Drain the potatoes and dry in a cloth until completely free of moisture. Clarify the butter in a small saucepan over a gentle heat. Mix the potatoes with the butter, salt and pepper in a large gratin dish, piling them up as loosely as possible. Cook in the oven for 20 minutes.

3   Take out of the oven and drain off the butter by tipping the dish and holding back the potatoes with a smaller dish. Put them back into the oven for 5 minutes so that they turn a good golden colour, drain off the extra butter again and serve very hot with fried or grilled meat.

Editor's note   These gaufrette potatoes are made with a wavy blade of a mandoline. To obtain the correct basketwork effect, slice the potato one way and then turn the potato 90° and slice again with the blade set at 3 mm ($\frac{1}{8}$ inch). Continue turning and slicing and the slices will come off looking like pieces of loose weaving, very pretty and very light.

Mother Carles' Potatoes

Pommes de terre 'Mère Carles'

For four people
Preparation time: 30 minutes
Cooking time: 35 minutes

Ingredients   1·5 kg (3 lb 6 oz) waxy potatoes
220 g (7¾ oz) smoked bacon, very thinly sliced to
    make 28 slices
80 g (2¾ oz) butter
salt, freshly-ground pepper

1   Peel the potatoes and, with a vegetable knife, cut into 28 large cylinders or corks 5 cm (2 in) long. Cut the bacon into 28 thin slices if you have not had this done for you in the shop.

2   Take a heavy sauté pan, large enough to hold all the potatoes side by side. Put in the potatoes, cover with cold salted water and bring to the boil to blanch them. Drain immediately in a colander.

3   Heat 50 g (1¾ oz) butter in the pan and, when it is a hazelnut brown, add the potatoes, season them with salt and cover the pan. Cook for about 20 minutes, shaking the pan frequently so that the potatoes gradually turn golden. Preheat the oven to 230° C/450° F/ Mark 8.

4   Take the pan off the heat, let the potatoes cool a little and then roll each one in a slice of bacon. Put them back into the pan side by side and cook in the oven for 10 minutes without covering.

5   Drain off the cooking fat, replace it with 30 g (1 oz) fresh butter and roll the potatoes in it. Arrange the potatoes in a serving dish and sprinkle each one with the butter, to make them glisten.

* These potatoes go very well with roast veal or with sautéed pork.

Editor's note   This dish would, of course, be delicious with small new potatoes in their skins.
Mère Carles, not to be confused with Mère Charles of Mionnay, is a doctor friend of the Troisgros who for sheer pleasure worked as a cook in their kitchen and invented this recipe.

Soufflé Potatoes in their Jackets

Pommes de terre en robe de chambre soufflées

For four people
Preparation time: 30 minutes
Cooking time: 1 hour

Ingredients 1 kg (2¼ lb) floury potatoes; choose 8 potatoes
of equal size and shape, weighing about 125 g
(4½ oz) each
50 g (1¾ oz) butter
5 tablespoons double cream
2 eggs
15 g (½ oz) chives
100 g (3½ oz) raw ham
salt, freshly-ground pepper

1   Preheat the oven to 200° C/400° F/Mark 6. Wash the potatoes carefully, rubbing the skins, and bake in the oven for 40 minutes.

2   Take them out of the oven and, with the point of a knife, cut through the skin all round the top of the potatoes. Discard the tops, which will not be used. Scoop out the inside of the potatoes with a spoon, put the cooked potato flesh into a sieve and press it through quickly to make a purée. Keep the empty potato skins hot.

3   Put the purée into a shallow saucepan and add the butter in little pieces, mixing it in briskly with a wooden spoon. In a separate pan, bring the cream to the boil and then add to the purée with a little salt and pepper. The result should be light and frothy.

4   Preheat the oven to 180° C/350° F/Mark 4. Separate the eggs and, off the heat, add the yolks, the chives, chopped at the last moment, and the ham cut into small dice to the potato purée. Whisk the whites of egg to a snow, but not too firm, and fold into the potato purée with a wooden spatula. Fill the potato skins to the top with the mixture, place on a baking sheet and cook in the oven for 15 minutes. Serve immediately.

* Arrange the potatoes on a white napkin in a heated dish.

Green Vegetable Purée

Purée de légumes Stéphanoise

For four people
Preparation time: 1 hour
Cooking time: 25 minutes

Ingredients

200 g (7 oz) petits pois, shelled
100 g (3½ oz) spinach leaves, with stalks removed
100 g (3½ oz) haricots verts
200 g (7 oz) asparagus tips, fresh when in season,
   or tinned
70 g (2½ oz) butter
½ teaspoon sugar
salt, freshly-ground pepper

Coupe-jarret (page 188)

Le grand dessert Troisgros (pages 254–5)

Terrine of Vegetables 'Olympe' – *Terrine de légumes 'Olympe'*
(page 100)

1   All the vegetables should be very fresh and should be prepared at the last moment. Cook them separately in the standard way, that is in plenty of boiling salted water, uncovered. Then refresh in cold water as quickly as possible. For the garnish, reserve a quarter of the peas, 24 asparagus tips and a fifth of the beans, cut into short lengths of 2 cm (1 in).

2   Put 30 g (1 oz) butter into a fairly large saucepan and sweat the spinach, covered, for 5 minutes. Then add the rest of the peas, beans and asparagus, cover the pan tightly and cook over a very low heat for just under 30 minutes.

3   Purée the hot vegetables in a sieve or mouli-légumes and return to the cleaned saucepan. Put the rest of the butter – 40 g ($1\frac{1}{2}$ oz) – into a very hot frying-pan, brown it lightly to a pale hazelnut colour and then pour it onto the purée. Stir for a few moments with a wooden spoon, add a pinch of sugar and taste for seasoning. If it has to be kept waiting, put the purée into a bain-marie and spread a few pieces of extra butter on top which, as they melt, will prevent a skin forming on the surface.

4   A few minutes before serving, put the purée in a vegetable dish. Heat the reserved vegetables in hot salted water, drain carefully and scatter over the purée.

(See editor's note on page 115)

Tomato Tomatoes

Tomates à la tomate

For four people
Preparation time: 20 minutes
Cooking time: 30 minutes

Ingredients   12 tomatoes, weighing about 1·5 kg (3 lb 6 oz)
        altogether
      2 onions
      1 clove of garlic, peeled
      1 sprig of thyme
      1 very small sprig of bayleaves
      a few parsley stalks
      15 g ($\frac{1}{2}$ oz) butter
      5 tablespoons arachide oil
      300 ml ($\frac{1}{2}$ pint) double cream
      salt, coarse and fine, freshly-ground pepper

1 Take 8 of the tomatoes and plunge them into a pan of boiling water for 30 seconds. Refresh them in cold water and skin. Cut them across in two, and squeeze them gently in the palm of your hand to remove the pips. Cut them into small even dice.

2 Chop the onions and crush the garlic. Prepare a bouquet garni with the herbs. Wash the 4 remaining tomatoes but don't peel them, cut them in half across and take out the pips.

3 In a small sauté pan, soften the onions in 10 g ($\frac{1}{3}$ oz) butter for 5 minutes without browning them. Add the diced tomatoes, the garlic, the bouquet garni and a few grains of coarse salt. Bring to the boil, cover the pan and let it cook for 25 minutes. Take out the bouquet garni, incorporate the rest of the butter and taste for seasoning. Preheat the oven to 180° C/350° F/Mark 4.

4 Season the tomato halves and sauté them in the hot oil in a round gratin dish, skin side up, for 5 minutes. Turn them over and finish cooking them in the oven for 10 minutes. Take them out, cover with the cream and let them simmer for a few minutes over a low heat.

5 Arrange the tomato halves on a serving dish, coat them lightly with the hot cream and fill them with the cooked tomatoes.

Pumpkin Fritters

Palets au potiron

For four people
Preparation time: 30 minutes
Cooking time: 1 minute

Ingredients   500 g (1 lb 2 oz) pumpkin
60 g (2 oz) flour
2 whole eggs
zest of 1 lemon, chopped
25 g (1 oz) butter
sugar
oil
salt, freshly-ground pepper

One day in advance

1   Peel the pumpkin and cut it into 4 pieces. Put it to cook in a large saucepan of boiling salted water for 15 to 30 minutes, depending on how ripe it is. Drain overnight in a cloth hanging over a bowl.

Preparing and cooking

2   Wring the cloth to squeeze out excess moisture and then press the pumpkin mixture into the pan in teaspoonfuls so that they processor. Put the purée into a mixing bowl with the flour, the eggs, the finely chopped lemon zest, 2 pinches of salt, a pinch of sugar and a turn of the peppermill. Clarify the butter in a small saucepan and slowly whisk it into the mixture in the bowl. Keep in a cool place.

3   Five minutes before serving, heat a lightly oiled frying-pan. Drop the pumpkin mixture into the pan in teaspoonfuls so that they spread and form little round flat shapes about 5 cm (2 in) in diameter, making sure that there is enough room for them to expand without touching each other. Cook for 30 seconds on each side and arrange in a ring on a serving dish.

* These fritters go well with spicy dishes or they can be dusted with sugar and eaten as a sweet.

Soufflé Chestnuts

Marrons en soufflé

For four people
Preparation time: 30 minutes
Cooking time: 14 minutes

Ingredients 300 g (10½ oz) chestnuts
butter and flour (for the soufflé dish)
200 ml (⅓ pint) milk
1 teaspoon sugar
2 tablespoons double cream
5 egg whites
3 egg yolks
salt

---

1   Choose large plump chestnuts. Peel them, following the method given for Chestnut Purée (page 248).

2   Butter and flour a soufflé dish 16 cm (6 in) in diameter and 6 cm (2¼ in) high, or four individual soufflé dishes 10 cm (4 in) in diameter and 5 cm (2 in) high. Preheat the oven to 180° C/350° F/Mark 4.

3   Cook the peeled and skinned chestnuts in a small saucepan with the milk, sugar and a pinch of salt. Cover the pan and boil for 10 minutes, then remove the lid and let them boil for another 5 minutes until at least half the milk has evaporated.

4   Reserve 4 whole chestnuts and purée the rest through a fine sieve. Return the purée to the pan, stir in the cream and leave just off the heat.

5   In a copper basin, using a hand whisk or a mixer, whisk the egg whites with a pinch of salt to a snow, whisking vigorously until they are very firm.

6   Add the egg yolks to the purée, stir for 1 minute and take off the heat. Then carefully mix in a quarter of the egg whites, crumble two of the whole chestnuts and stir them in. With a wooden spatula, fold the rest of the whites into the purée, cutting the mixture across the middle and turning it over to bring the mixture from the bottom up to the top. The lightness of the whole soufflé depends on the skill and speed with which you do this.

7   Turn the mixture into the soufflé dish or dishes, smooth the surface with the spatula and strew with the two remaining chestnuts, cut into 12 pieces. Put in the oven and cook for 14 minutes or less for small soufflés. Serve at once.

Chestnut Purée

Purée mauve

For four people
Preparation time: 45 minutes
Cooking time: 25 minutes

Ingredients 1 kg (2¼ lb) chestnuts
500 ml (scant pint) milk
1 tablespoon cognac
100 g (3½ oz) butter
sugar, salt

1   Preheat the oven to 220° C/425° F/Mark 7. With the point of a knife, slit the sides of the chestnuts without cutting right into them. Spread them on a baking sheet and put into the oven for 7 to 8 minutes. Then peel off the shell and the furry inner skin with a knife.

2   Put the chestnuts into a saucepan, cover with the milk, put the lid on the pan and let them cook gently for 25 minutes. Then press through a sieve with what little liquid is left.

3   Return the purée to the cleaned saucepan and heat through, stirring with a wooden spoon. A few seconds before serving, mix in the cognac and the butter in small nuts. Taste and season with salt and sugar as necessary.

* This purée is meant to be eaten with game and roast pork.

Vegetable Spirals

Serpentins de légumes

For four people
Preparation time: 45 minutes
Cooking time: 8 minutes

Ingredients
2 turnips, weighing 200 g (7 oz) each
2 carrots, weighing 200 g (7 oz) each
1 cucumber weighing 100 g (3½ oz)
100 g (3½ oz) butter
salt, freshly-ground pepper

1 Use large vegetables for this dish. Cut the turnips into 2 cylinders 6 cm (2¼ in) long and trim them. Using a very sharp, fine-bladed knife, peel off as long a ribbon as possible round each cylinder. Don't worry if it breaks because it can still be used. Repeat this operation with the carrots, first blanching them whole for 3 minutes to make them more flexible, and then with the cucumber, cutting down to the pips.

2 Plunge the vegetable ribbons carefully into boiling water for one minute, take them out with a skimmer and let them cool. Put the different ribbons together to form three-coloured strips 20 to 25 cm (8 to 10 in) long. Then roll them together and tie them up with two pieces of string. Cook in salted boiling water for 8 minutes.

3 Put 2¼ tablespoons water in a small saucepan, bring it to the boil and, over a brisk heat, whisk in the butter, cut into small pieces, until completely emulsified. Season with salt and pepper.

4 Take the vegetable coils out of the water and place them round the edges of four hot plates, preferably white to show off the colours of the vegetables. Unroll one third of each little coil, spreading the ends out so that they look like ribbons blowing in the wind. Coat them lightly with the melted butter sauce and serve at once.

Editor's note The trick to this recipe is to imagine you are peeling an apple in a continuous spiral.

Noodles with Bacon

Nouilles au lard

For four people
Preparation time: 30 minutes
Cooking time: 15 minutes

Ingredients 200 g (7 oz) green streaky bacon
500 g (1 lb 2 oz) tomatoes
300 g (10½ oz) fresh noodles (tagliatelle)
8 mint leaves
2 cloves of garlic, peeled and chopped
salt, freshly-ground pepper

1 Take off the rind and cut the bacon into little lardons. Blanch them in a pan of boiling water and drain well.

2 Plunge the tomatoes into boiling water, skin them, cut them in two across and squeeze out the pips and excess moisture. Press the tomato pulp through a fine sieve.

3 If you don't want the bother of making the noodles, they can be bought ready-made in Italian delicatessens. Weigh 30 g (1 oz), and cut them into short lengths of 3 cm ($1\frac{1}{2}$ in).

4 Boil the tomato pulp in a small saucepan for 5 minutes, together with the mint, which should be taken out at the end, and the chopped garlic.

5 Sauté the lardons in a frying-pan until golden and set them aside with half their cooking fat. Then sauté the short lengths of noodles in the remaining fat for 3 minutes. Cook the rest in a large saucepan of boiling salted water, maintaining a steady boil for 7 to 8 minutes. Pour in a glass of cold water to stop them cooking and drain immediately. The pasta should be cooked at the last moment and dressed just before serving.

6 After draining them thoroughly, return the noodles to the pan in which they cooked. Pour on the tomato sauce and the lardons with their fat and mix everything well with a fork. Turn into a bowl and scatter the fried noodles over the top.

Pasta with Truffles

Coquillettes aux truffes 'Jolly Martine'

For four people
Preparation time: 15 minutes
Cooking time: 14 minutes

Ingredients 40 g (1½ oz) truffles, thinly pared, with their juice
180 g (6¼ oz) pasta shells
100 g (3½ oz) butter
salt

---

1 If you can get fresh truffles (in January and February), steam them slowly for 20 minutes with a little salted water in a covered pan. If you buy preserved ones, try to obtain the best quality. In either case, trim them and cut them into even julienne strips. Reserve 2½ tablespoons to ¼ pint of the truffle juice, depending on how concentrated it is.

2 Choose small pasta shells, preferably made with eggs. Heat 2 litres (3½ pints) salted water in a large saucepan and, as soon as it comes to the boil, add the shells and stir so that they don't stick together. Cook uncovered for 12 to 14 minutes, then pour in a glass of cold water to stop them cooking and drain in a colander.

3 In a medium-sized pan, reduce the truffle juice until almost completely evaporated and add the pasta and the butter cut in small pieces. Stir with a two-pronged kitchen fork so that the pasta shells are coated with the melted butter. Stir in the truffle julienne without breaking them and serve at once.

Editor's note This recipe is named for Martine Jolly, cookery writer and wife of the French gastronome and writer Claude Jolly.
For the method of steaming truffles, see page 233.

Desserts

Le grand dessert Troisgros

This dessert consists of a variety of different fruits, changing with the seasons. It is imperative to have as wide an assortment as possible of the freshest, best quality fruit. It is served with freshly made ice-creams and sorbets, and sprinkled at the last moment with a sauce of fresh raspberries and perhaps crème fraîche.

To prepare the poached fruits

The syrup: The proportions are 600 to 700 g (1 lb 7 oz to 1 lb 9 oz) sugar per litre (1¾ pints) water and it should cover the fruit completely. The cooking time will vary according to the ripeness of the fruit.

Peaches: Skin them and poach in syrup. White peaches should be left whole; yellow peaches should be cut in half and have their stones removed.

Pears: Peel them and rub with a cut lemon, leaving the stalk on and carefully removing the core and pips. Poach in syrup. Cut very large ones in half.

Cherries: Poach them quickly in the syrup with a few of the stones pounded and tied in a muslin bag.

Apricots: Cut in half and poach in syrup with a cinnamon stick.

Mirabelle plums: Poach whole in syrup.

Prunes: Poach (for the method, see page 183).

Figs: Poach in red wine with sugar and bayleaves.

To prepare the raw fruits

New season's almonds: Shell and skin them, and split in two.

Grapes: Peel them and remove the pips.

Melon and water melon: Remove the seeds and use a melon baller to scoop out the flesh, taking care not to go too near the skin. Let them marinate in sugar and orange liqueur.

Pineapple: Peel it, cut into small segments and marinate in cold syrup.

Oranges, grapefruit: Peel off all the skin and pith, leaving the flesh completely exposed. Insert a small sharp knife into each segment between the flesh and the skin separating it from its neighbour and slice into the centre of the fruit. Do this on both sides in order to obtain segments of flesh completely free of skin. Let them marinate for 24 hours in sugar and their own juice.

To prepare soft fruits

Strawberries: Remove the stalks and wash if necessary, sprinkle with sugar and lemon juice. Cut the largest ones in half.
Wild strawberries, raspberries, blackberries and mulberries need no preparation.

Sauce of fresh raspberries (for four people)

Take 200 g (7 oz) raspberries and sieve in a mouli-légumes. Put the purée into a glass bowl, add 140 g (5 oz) sugar and keep in a cool place, stirring from time to time with a wooden spoon to dissolve the sugar. Out of season, you can use frozen raspberries with good results.

Designing the dish

Take a large, very cold plate and in the centre place 1 rounded table-spoon of a fresh fruit sorbet (prickly pear – page 263; strawberry; raspberry; pineapple) and 1 tablespoon ice-cream (walnut – page 262; vanilla; honey). Arrange the seasonal fruits prettily around the dish, taking care to balance the colours. Sprinkle them delicately with the fresh raspberry sauce, or with a thin thread of cream (but very little or none at all).

In a separate dish, offer tiny helpings of different cakes and pastries, such as Clafoutis with Kiwis (page 264), Reinette Apple Pudding (page 268), Triple-tiered Chocolate Cake (page 276), or a gooseberry mille-feuille. Decorate the table with Opus Incertum (page 280), Almond Tiles (page 282), Pamélas (page 260), marrons glacés and macaroons soaked in different liqueurs and flavourings.

(see colour illustration between pages 224 and 225)

Prunes in Dessert Wine with Cream

Pruneaux au Rasteau et à la crème fraîche

For four people
Preparation time: 15 minutes
Cooking time: 10 minutes

Ingredients

36 prunes
500 ml (scant pint) dessert wine (preferably Rasteau from the Rhône valley)
500 ml (scant pint) light red Bordeaux
1 orange
1 lemon
100 g ($3\frac{1}{2}$ oz) caster sugar
200 ml ($\frac{1}{3}$ pint) raspberry juice
200 ml ($\frac{1}{3}$ pint) double cream

Four days before

1 Soak the prunes in the dessert wine and the red wine and leave them to marinate overnight.

2 The next day, when the prunes are nice and plump, put them into a saucepan with their wine. Add the sugar, raspberry juice and the unpeeled orange and lemon, cut into thick slices. Bring to the boil and simmer for 15 minutes. Steep the prunes for 3 days in their cooking liquid in a cool place.

Serving

3 Remove the slices of orange and lemon and serve the prunes in deep bowls with their juice. Pour double cream all over the top.

Editor's note A wine similar to Rasteau and more readily available in Britain is Beaumes-de-Venise, another 'vin doux naturel', made from the muscat grape in the region just south of Rasteau.
Raspberry juice is obtained by pressing raspberries, fresh or frozen, through a sieve.

Peaches and Almonds in Beaujolais

Pêches et amandes au Brouilly

For four people
Preparation time: 30 minutes

Ingredients   10 white peaches, about 1 kg (2¼ lb) altogether
24 new season's almonds
250 ml (scant half pint) Beaujolais (preferably Brouilly)
200 g (7 oz) fresh raspberries
150 g (5¼ oz) sugar

1   Peel the peaches with a small stainless steel kitchen knife, which is easy to do if they are really ripe. Cut each into 8 slices, cutting from the outside to the stone, and put the slices in a bowl.

2   Shell the almonds and then plunge them for 2 minutes into boiling water, refresh in cold water and press between your fingers to remove the skin. Divide the two halves of each kernel by inserting the point of a knife in between.

3   Purée the raspberries quickly through a sieve placed over a bowl. Add the Beaujolais and pour over the peaches, sprinkle with the sugar and keep in a cool place for about 1 hour.

4   Cool four large Burgundy glasses and divide the peaches between them. Sprinkle with the halved almonds and eat with dessertspoons.

* If you don't have really large glasses, you can serve the peaches in little cocottes embedded in a layer of crushed ice.

Tango Oranges

Oranges tango

For four people
Preparation time: 1 hour
Cooking time: 1 hour

Ingredients   8 oranges
2½ tablespoons Grand Marnier
10 g (⅓ oz) caster sugar
5 tablespoons grenadine

Three hours in advance

1   Choose seedless oranges which have not been artificially preserved, for instance Spanish navel oranges available from November to April. Wash them and peel thinly with a potato peeler, being careful to take off just the zest without any pith on it. Cut the peel into even julienne strips and blanch in boiling water for 15 minutes. Refresh in cold water and drain.

2   With a vegetable knife, strip the oranges of the white pith and, over a bowl, separate the segments by slicing between the membrane and flesh, letting them fall, one by one, into the bowl. Squeeze the juice from the membranes over the orange segments, add the Grand Marnier and the sugar, and leave to marinate in a cool place for at least 3 hours.

One hour in advance

3   Bring the grenadine to the boil in a saucepan, add the orange peel julienne and cook over a gentle heat until the liquid has evaporated and the peel has turned into a soft jam and tangled into a mass. This will take between 45 and 60 minutes.

Serving

4   Serve the oranges in individual glasses with the peel 'confit' on top.

259

Pamélas

For four people
Preparation time: 30 minutes
Cooking time: 1 hour 30 minutes

Ingredients   6 grapefruit, weighing about 2 kg (4 lb 6 oz) altogether
600 g (1 lb 5 oz) caster sugar
100 g (3½ oz) granulated sugar

1   Choose thick-skinned grapefruit and slice off both ends. Stand the grapefruits on end and quarter them, then remove two thirds of the flesh from the middle of each quarter, leaving the remaining third attached to the skin. Then cut each quarter downwards into 4 long strips, which will give you 96 sticks 7 cm (3 in) long and 1·5 cm ($\frac{1}{2}$ in) thick.

2   Put the strips into a saucepan, cover with cold water and bring very slowly to the boil. Simmer for 5 minutes and drain. Repeat the blanching four times, to remove much of the bitterness of the fruit.

3   After they have been drained for the fifth time, return the strips to the pan, without water this time but with the caster sugar. Cook them very slowly, uncovered, on a low heat for between 50 and 60 minutes, stirring often with a wooden spatula. If the evaporation is too fast, the zest will not be properly cooked.

4   Spread out the slices to dry on a rack and, when they are cold, roll them one by one in the granulated sugar. Serve cold.

* These are extremely good with very lightly sugared coffee.

* You can use up the middle parts of the grapefruit for breakfast the next morning. With a very sharp little kitchen knife, slice between each bit of membrane to separate the segments. Take out the pips, and put the flesh into a bowl. Sprinkle generously with sugar and leave to marinate overnight in a cold place. Serve at breakfast in small glass bowls.

Walnut Ice-cream

Glace aux noix

For four people
Preparation time: 40 minutes
Cooking time: 10 minutes

Ingredients 50 g (1¾ oz) fresh walnuts, shelled
500 ml (scant pint) milk
5 egg yolks
100 g (3½ oz) acacia honey
1 tablespoon walnut liqueur

1 Choose whole fresh walnuts, crack open the shells, take out the kernels, weigh them and then peel them with a small sharp knife. Chop them up roughly on a board. Bring the milk to the boil in a saucepan, add the walnuts and leave to infuse for 10 minutes just off the heat.

2 Mix the egg yolks with the honey in a bowl and beat with a whisk for at least 5 minutes. Transfer to a saucepan, pour on the infusion with its walnuts and stir continuously over a gentle heat with a wooden spatula. As soon as the mixture begins to thicken slightly and coats the spatula, take off the heat. It absolutely must not boil.

3 Pour the mixture into a bowl and refrigerate. Then add the walnut liqueur. Just before serving, and no more than 30 minutes in advance, put the mixture into an electric ice-cream maker and freeze.

Editor's note If you do not have an electric ice-cream maker – a sorbetière – you must whisk the ice-cream two or three times as it sets, to break down the ice-crystals to a fine-grained consistency. However, if you like making ice-creams and sorbets, a 'sorbetière' is a very good investment, giving a much better texture than the hand method, and being so troublefree that you can make a simple fresh fruit sorbet or an ice-cream in a few minutes.

Prickly Pear Sorbet

Sorbet à la figue de Barbarie

For four people
Preparation time: 30 minutes

Ingredients   1·3 kg (2 lb 14 oz) prickly pears
150 g (5¼ oz) caster sugar
1 tablespoon kirsch
juice of 1 lemon
2 tablespoons whipping cream

1   The prickly pears should be perfectly ripe. It is essential to wear gloves when you peel them to avoid contact with the small prickles dotted about on the skin. Cut off both ends with a vegetable knife, and make an incision from top to bottom so that you can peel off the skin easily. Cut 4 of the fruits into slices 2 cm (¾ in) thick and put them aside in a bowl, sprinkled with 20 g (¾ oz) sugar and with the kirsch. Purée the rest through the mouli-légumes placed over a bowl, add the lemon juice and 65 g (2¼ oz) sugar, and set aside in a cool place.

2   Set a large bowl in a bed of crushed ice, put in the cream and whisk for about 5 minutes so that it is thick but very light. Mix in the rest of the sugar – 65 g (2¼ oz) – and then fold carefully into the fruit purée. Freeze the mixture in an electric ice-cream maker.

3   Serve in scoops in an earthenware bowl and arrange the slices of prickly pear on top.

Clafoutis with Kiwis

Clafoutis aux kiwis

For eight people
Preparation time: 30 minutes
Cooking time: 30 minutes

Ingredients   10 kiwi fruits
200 g (7 oz) sweet flan pastry (page 35)
4 eggs
250 ml ($\frac{1}{3}$ pint) double cream
150 g (5$\frac{1}{4}$ oz) icing sugar
2 tablespoons eau-de-vie de prune (plum
    liqueur)

1   Peel the kiwi fruits and cut into slices 1 cm ($\frac{1}{2}$ in) thick. Preheat the oven to 200° C/400° F/Mark 6. Butter a 25 cm (10 in) flan ring placed on a baking sheet and line it with the flan pastry, prick the base all over with a fork, cover with a sheet of greaseproof paper, fill with dried beans and bake blind in the oven for 10 minutes.

2   Prepare the filling. Put the whole eggs, the cream, 100 g (3$\frac{1}{2}$ oz) sugar and the eau-de-vie into a bowl and mix with a whisk. Then strain through a fine conical strainer.

3   Take the pastry out of the oven (it is only half cooked at this stage), remove the paper and the beans and arrange the slices of kiwi over the bottom. Cover with the filling and return to the oven to cook for 20 minutes at 180° C/350° F/Mark 4.

4   Take the flan out of the oven, protect the edges with paper, sprinkle the top with the rest of the sugar and put under the grill until the surface is covered with little beads of caramel. Slide the clafoutis onto a dish and remove the flan ring.

Blueberries in a Cabbage-leaf Tart

Gouïre aux myrtilles dans la feuille de chou

For four people
Preparation time: 25 minutes
Cooking time: 20 minutes

Ingredients   3 cabbage leaves
2 eggs
20 g ($\frac{3}{4}$ oz) flour
70 g ($2\frac{1}{2}$ oz) sugar
2 tablespoons double cream
160 g ($5\frac{1}{2}$ oz) blueberries **or** bilberries
20 g ($\frac{3}{4}$ oz) butter

1   Preheat the oven to 170° C/325° F/Mark 3. Choose three good cabbage leaves, remove the thickest part of the stalks and ribs and blanch them for 10 minutes in plenty of boiling water, slightly salted.

2   Mix the eggs, flour, sugar and cream in a bowl and strain through a fine conical strainer.

3   Pick over the berries and throw out any leaves and small branches.

4   Heat a round copper or enamelled iron gratin dish about 20 cm (8 in) in diameter, melt the butter and roll the cabbage leaves in it. Then spread them round the base and sides of the pan, fill with the berries and pour in the egg and cream mixture. Cook in the oven for 15 minutes.

5   Take it out of the oven and finish cooking over the heat, so that the cabbage becomes a nice golden colour. Check to see how it is doing by lifting the leaves slightly with a spatula.

6   Gently slide the tart onto a heated dish, leave for about 15 minutes and eat warm.

Editor's note   This dish is a variation of a regional recipe from the neighbourhood of Roanne and is borrowed from André Delorme, pâtissier at Les Frères Troisgros.

Cherry Pastries Lamartine

Coffret de cerises Lamartine

For four people
Preparation time: 20 minutes
Cooking time: 5 minutes

Ingredients 60 cherries, ripe but firm
200 ml ($\frac{1}{3}$ pint) redcurrant jelly
2$\frac{1}{2}$ tablespoons old kirsch
400 g (14 oz) rectangular brioche loaf (baked in a tin)
icing sugar

1   Stone the cherries with a cherry stoner or, better, with a piece of wire, bent over (like a hairpin) and stuck in a cork. Melt the red-currant jelly in a shallow pan, dilute with 5 tablespoons water and bring to the boil. Throw in the cherries, cover the pan and let it cook for 5 minutes over a high heat.

2   Take off the heat and remove the cherries from the syrup with a slotted spoon. Put them into a dish. Reduce the syrup until it becomes a jelly and you have about 200 ml ($\frac{1}{3}$ pint). Away from the heat, add the kirsch, which should not boil if it is to preserve its aroma.

3   Cut the brioche into slices 2 cm (1 in) thick, and trim the edges to give rectangles of about 7 cm (3 in) by 12 cm (5 in). With the point of a small knife, cut a smaller rectangle 1 cm ($\frac{1}{2}$ in) from the edges in one side, so that you have a 'lid' which can be lifted off after the slices have been glazed. Place them on a baking sheet, dust with the icing sugar and put them to caramelise under a hot grill. Turn them over, dust the other sides with sugar, and glaze.

4   Carefully remove the 'lids' from the brioche cases. Divide the syrup between four shallow bowls, put the glazed brioche cases on top, fill with the cherries, replace the lids and serve.

* This dish should be served lukewarm.

Editor's note   This dish was created for Martine who worked for the Troisgros brothers.

Reinette Apple Pudding

Gâteau aux pommes reinettes

For four people
Preparation time: 1 hour
Cooking time: 40 minutes

Ingredients 1·5 kg (3 lb 6 oz) Reinette apples (Coxes or rus-
sets will do)
160 g (5½ oz) sugar
3 eggs
50 g (1¾ oz) butter
juice of ¼ lemon
4 slices of white bread
icing sugar

1   Choose ripe apples, peel them and cut into four, discarding the core and pips. Put them to cook in a covered saucepan over a moderate heat for 45 minutes, stirring occasionally. Take off the lid, add 100 g (3½ oz) sugar and continue to cook, stirring with a wooden spoon, until the apples are thick enough to stand up in a mound. Take off the heat and purée through a sieve. Beat the eggs and add to the purée with the softened butter, working everything together with a spatula.

2   Put the remaining sugar – 60 g (2 oz) – into a fireproof mould 25 cm (10 in) in diameter, with a few drops of lemon juice and 1 tablespoon water. Place on the heat and caramelise, shaking all the time. When the caramel is a clear brown, after about 10 minutes, tip the mould slightly to coat the sides.

3   Cut 8 heart shapes out of the slices of bread and arrange them side by side in the bottom of the mould in the form of a rosette, turning them over in the caramel to colour them on both sides, then fill the mould with the apple purée and cook in a bain-marie for 40 minutes at 160° C/310° F/between Mark 2 and 3. Let the pudding cool slightly and turn it out of the mould. If the top is not a pretty, deep golden colour, sprinkle it with icing sugar and glaze it under a hot grill.

* This pudding can be eaten lukewarm or cold with crème anglaise.

Editor's note   Crème anglaise is the classic custard sauce made with egg yolks, sugar and milk and flavoured with vanilla – it is no relation of packet custard – and is served when something less rich than cream is needed.

Rhubarb Tart with Cream

Tarte à la rhubarbe à la crème

For four people
Preparation time: 30 minutes
Cooking time: 30 minutes

Ingredients   600 g (1 lb 5 oz) rhubarb, weighing about 400 g
(14 oz) when trimmed and peeled
170 g (6 oz) caster sugar
zest of $\frac{1}{2}$ lemon, chopped
150 g ($5\frac{1}{4}$ oz) sweet flan pastry (page 35)
3 tablespoons double cream, chilled
2 cloves, crushed

1 Cut the trimmed rhubarb into pieces 15 cm (6 in) long and peel off the stringy bits. Then slice as thinly as possible.

2 Put the rhubarb into a saucepan with 160 g (5½ oz) sugar, seal tightly and let it stew gently for 10 minutes. Take off the lid and put the pan over brisk heat, stirring with a wooden spatula until all the moisture has evaporated and the rhubarb has the consistency of an apple purée. Add the chopped lemon zest.

3 Preheat the oven to 200°C/400°F/Mark 6. Take a flan ring 15 cm (6 in) in diameter and line with the pastry. Prick the base with a fork, line with greaseproof paper, fill with dried beans and bake blind for 10 minutes.

4 Remove the paper and beans and fill the tart with the rhubarb. Cook in the oven at 150°C/300°F/Mark 2 for 15 minutes. Take out the flan, place it on a rack and allow to cool.

5 Pour the chilled cream into a bowl and lightly whip with a whisk until it is firm but light. Mix in 10 g (⅓ oz) sugar and the crushed cloves. Spread the cream over the rhubarb, smooth it with a spatula and trace a little pattern on the top. Serve as soon as possible.

* Choose, if possible, rhubarb stalks from the heart of the plant. You can tell if they are ripe by the deep red colour along the edges.

Melon Tart

Tarte au melon

For four people
Preparation time: 30 minutes
Cooking time: 20 minutes

Ingredients   175 g (6 oz) sweet flan pastry (page 35)
3 melons, weighing 600 g (1 lb 5 oz) each
juice of $\frac{1}{4}$ lemon
3 leaves of gelatine, weighing 5 g ($\frac{1}{4}$ oz) each
25 g (1 oz) caster sugar

1 To make the pastry case, follow the instructions for Clafoutis with Kiwis (page 264), but bake blind for the whole cooking time, that is for 25 to 30 minutes altogether. Protect the edges with a strip of aluminium foil if they seem to be getting too brown. Allow to cool.

2 Choose melons which are ripe, but not overripe, heavy in the hand and with a good scent. Cut the first melon in half, carefully scoop out the seeds and, with a melon-baller, make 24 little balls to decorate the flan. Scoop out the rest of the flesh, without scraping the skin, and purée it quickly through a sieve into a bowl. Add the lemon juice and keep in a cool place.

3 Soak the gelatine in cold water. Cut the two other melons into four and scoop out the flesh, transferring it to a saucepan. Add the sugar and cook for about 10 minutes, stirring with a wooden spoon so that the moisture evaporates. Drain the gelatine and add to the melon purée, making sure that it is completely dissolved. Remove from the heat, and when the mixture is cold, add the uncooked melon purée and lemon juice.

4 Fill the cooked and cooled pastry case with the mixture and chill in the refrigerator for 2 hours. Decorate with the reserved melon balls and serve very cold.

Editor's note This is a recipe for a scorching hot day. It should be eaten not more than two hours after it is made or it will not give a nice contrast of crisp pastry and cool fresh melon purée.

Pumpkin Pudding

Millet au potiron

For four people
Preparation time: 30 minutes
Cooking time: 40 minutes

Ingredients
1 pumpkin weighing 700 g (1 lb 9 oz)
40 g (1½ oz) currants
20 g (¾ oz) butter
50 g (1¾ oz) flour
50 g (1¾ oz) sugar
3 eggs
250 ml (scant half pint) milk
2½ tablespoon double cream
3 strips of lemon peel
nutmeg, freshly-ground pepper, salt

1   Choose a good ripe pumpkin, preferably of a bright orange. Peel it and cut into large pieces. Soak the currants in cold water.

2   Put the pieces of pumpkin into a saucepan of slightly salted boiling water, and cook for 10 minutes. Drain in a colander. Melt the butter in a frying-pan, put the pumpkin in and sauté until all the moisture has evaporated and it has melted to a purée.

3   Preheat the oven to 170° C/325° F/Mark 3. Put the flour, sugar, whole eggs, milk and cream in a large bowl and mix with a whisk for a few moments. Then stir in the pumpkin purée and add the drained currants, a little grated nutmeg, a turn of the peppermill and the strips of lemon peel.

4   Take a fairly large gratin dish, so that the pudding will be between 4 and 5 cm ($1\frac{1}{2}$ and 2 in) thick. Pour in the mixture and cook in a bain-marie in the pre-heated oven for 40 minutes. Then put into the refrigerator for 2 to 3 hours and serve well chilled.

Triple-tiered Chocolate Cake

Le trois-tiers au chocolat

For eight people
Preparation time: 1 hour 30 minutes
Cooking time: 30 minutes

---

* This cake is a Genoese filled with chocolate mousse and whipped cream.

Ingredients   *for the Genoese mixture:*
4 eggs
125 g (4¼ oz) sugar
125 g (4¼ oz) cornflour
25 g (1 oz) unsweetened cocoa powder
20 g (¾ oz) butter (to grease the mould)
flour

for the chocolate mousse:
125 g (4¼ oz) couverture (cooking chocolate)
3 tablespoons milk
25 g (1 oz) caster sugar
2 eggs, separated

for the whipped cream:
500 ml (scant pint) whipping cream
20 g (¾ oz) sugar

for the decoration:
80 g (2¾ oz) flaked almonds
50 g (2 oz) plain chocolate

Preparing the chocolate mousse

Twelve hours in advance

1 Melt the chocolate in the milk over a very low heat and mix in the sugar and the egg yolks, stirring continuously. Let it cool to room temperature, whisk the egg whites to a snow and fold them lightly but thoroughly into the chocolate mixture with a wooden spatula. Keep in a cool place for at least 12 hours.

Preparing the Genoese

2 Preheat the oven to 160°C/310°F/Mark 2 to 3. Put a sauté pan into a bain-marie of warm water on the edge of the heat and in it whip the whole eggs and the sugar with a whisk, until the volume has increased by a third. The mixture should be just warm and form a ribbon as it runs from the spatula. Add the cornflour and the cocoa powder and mix everything together thoroughly.

3 Butter and flour a mould, 25 cm (10 in) in diameter and 5 cm (2 in) deep, pour in the mixture and cook in the oven for 30 minutes. Take the cake out of the oven, turn it onto a rack and allow it to cool.

Preparing the whipped cream

4 Pour the cream into a chilled bowl and whisk for about 7 to 8 minutes. As soon as it thickens, add the sugar and mix it in lightly. Keep in a cool place.

Assembling the cake

5 Divide the cake horizontally into three equal parts with a bread knife. Place the bottom slice on a piece of card cut to the same size and cover with two thirds of the chocolate mousse. Put the second layer on top and spread with the whipped cream. Then complete the cake with the third layer and cover the top and the sides with the rest of the chocolate mousse.

6 Toast the flaked almonds under the grill, shaking them until they are a lovely golden colour. Then, holding the cake up on one hand, press them all round the sides of the cake with the other. Put the cake down and using a potato peeler, shave off thin curls of chocolate letting them fall over the top of the cake.

Oreillettes

For four people
Preparation time: 30 minutes
Cooking time: 3 minutes

Ingredients   250 g (8¾ oz) flour
100 g (3½ oz) caster sugar
2 egg yolks
40 g (1½ oz) butter, softened
1 tablespoon rum
zest of ½ lemon, grated
1 litre (1¾ pints) olive oil

One hour in advance

1 Put the flour in a mound on your work surface, preferably a marble top, and make a well in the centre. Put 75 g (2½ oz) sugar, the 2 egg yolks, the softened butter, the rum and the lemon peel in the well, and mix them together with the fingertips of one hand, without touching the flour. Then add ½ tablespoon cold water and gradually incorporate with the flour, without handling it too much or it will become heavy and elastic. Roll it into a ball, cover with a damp cloth and allow to rest for 1 hour in a cool place.

Preparation

2 Roll out the pastry on your worktop to a thickness of 5 mm (¼ in). Roll out and repeat the operation so that the pastry has had two folds and ends up 5 mm (¼ in) thick. Cut into diamond shapes 10 cm (4 in) long and 5 cm (2 in) across and mark out a pattern on each one with the back of a knife. The traditional patterns are geometric designs of criss-crossed lines.

Cooking and serving

3 Heat the olive oil in a deep frying-pan to 180°C/350°F and plunge the pastries into the oil for 2 to 3 minutes. Drain them on a napkin and sprinkle with the rest of the sugar.

* These pastries should be eaten cold and can be kept for 2 to 3 days in a cake tin.

Editor's note If it seems too extravagant to use olive oil for frying, substitute sunflower oil or arachide oil – the flavour will not be quite the same but still very good.

Opus Incertum

For 10 people
Preparation time: 20 minutes
Cooking time: 20 minutes

Ingredients   200 g (7 oz) flaky pastry (page 36)
80 g (2¾ oz) caster sugar
10 g (⅓ oz) icing sugar

Editor's note   'Opus incertum' is the name given to a particular method of laying tiles. Whereas in 'opus cathedra' the tiles are arranged in a check pattern and in 'opus romanum' in a brickwork pattern, in 'opus incertum' they are arranged without any particular regularity, hence the name of this dish.

1 Use pastry made the previous day, which has had four folds. Cover your work surface with 30 g (1 oz) caster sugar and give the pastry its fifth fold. Then cover the surface with another 30 g (1 oz) sugar before giving the sixth fold. In this way, the sugar, rather than the usual flour, becomes incorporated into the pastry. Let the pastry rest in the refrigerator for 20 minutes.

2 Using the remaining 20 g ($\frac{3}{4}$ oz) caster sugar, roll out the pastry into a rectangle 15 cm (6 in) wide. Then divide the rectangle lengthwise into three, to give three strips 5 cm (2 in) wide. Moisten these with water, using a pastry brush, put them on top of each other and press down lightly with the rolling-pin so that they stick together. Put them on a plate and leave in the freezer to chill for 15 minutes.

3 Preheat the oven to 150° C/300° F/Mark 2. Cover a baking sheet with silicone baking paper, dust it with the icing sugar and sprinkle lightly with water. Cut the pastry strips into sticks 5 mm (no more than $\frac{1}{4}$ in) thick. Arrange them flat on the sheet in staggered rows, leaving a space of 2 to 3 cm ($\frac{3}{4}$ to 1 in) between each one. Put into the oven, turn it off and cook for 10 minutes, then relight the oven and cook for another 10 minutes. The pastry will expand sideways as it cooks and the sugar will caramelise and join the whole thing together, so that it looks like crazy paving. Let the pastry cool on the sheet for 30 minutes.

4 Put a white napkin into a large silver dish and carefully turn the pastry into it. Place in the middle of the table so that your guests can break off pieces of the 'opus' with their fingers.

Almond Tiles

La grosse tuile

For four people
Preparation time: 15 minutes
Cooking time: 10 minutes

Ingredients 30 g (1 oz) butter
130 g (4½ oz) flaked almonds
120 g (4¼ oz) caster sugar
20 g (¾ oz) flour
5 tablespoons whites of egg (about 2½ whites)

At least two hours in advance

1   Melt 20 g ($\frac{3}{4}$ oz) butter without letting it get too hot. Set aside 10 g ($\frac{1}{3}$ oz) flaked almonds.

2   Mix the remaining almonds, caster sugar and flour together in a bowl. Add the whites of egg and the melted butter, stirring all the time. Let the mixture rest for at least 2 hours or, preferably, overnight.

Cooking

3   Preheat the oven to 170°C/325°F/Mark 3. Butter a baking sheet, take a quarter of the mixture and spread it in the pan with a fork dipped in cold water, to give an oval 15 cm (6 in) by 20 cm (8 in). It should be an even thickness all over, so that it cooks evenly. Strew the surface with a few of the reserved almonds and cook in the oven for 10 minutes. Keep an eye on it and take it out when it is a pleasant brown all over.

Finishing and serving

4   As soon as you have taken it out of the oven, roll the biscuit round an empty bottle, with the longest side along the length of the bottle, and leave on its side to cool.

5   Repeat the whole operation three times with the remaining mixture and almonds – unless you have an oven large enough to cook several at once.

6   When they are cold, pick up the biscuits very carefully and arrange them on a large dish.

* Serve, if you like, with petits fours.

Praline Soufflé

Soufflé flambé aux pralines

For four people
Preparation time: 45 minutes
Cooking time: 16 minutes

Ingredients

10 g ($\frac{1}{3}$ oz) butter
20 g ($\frac{3}{4}$ oz) caster sugar
150 g ($5\frac{1}{4}$ oz) pralines
3 egg yolks
6 tablespoons crème pâtissière (page 288)
8 egg whites
2 tablespoons orange liqueur
a pinch of salt

1   Butter a 30 cm (12 in) gratin dish and coat the inside with the sugar, shaking the dish from side to side and then turning it over to shake out the excess.

2   Crush the pralines coarsely with a rolling-pin on your worktop.

3   Add the 3 egg yolks to the warm crème pâtissière, whisking them in for 2 to 3 minutes.

4   Preheat the oven to 180°C/350°F/Mark 4. Season the egg whites with a pinch of salt and whisk to a snow in a copper bowl. When they are firm, mix a quarter of them into the crème pâtissière. Then pour this onto the rest of the whites and fold them together with a wooden spatula. Add the pralines, keeping back one fifth. Turn the mixture into the prepared gratin dish, smooth the top with the spatula and sprinkle with the rest of the pralines.

5   Stand the dish for 1 minute on a very hot baking sheet and then cook in the oven for 16 minutes.

6   Bring the soufflé quickly to the table, sprinkle with the liqueur and flame the soufflé, making little slits in the surface so that the alcohol penetrates to the inside. Serve immediately and accompany with praline ice-cream.

Editor's note   Pralines are almonds coated with caramel. If you cannot buy them, they can be made at home. Throw toasted blanched almonds into a saucepan of caramel while still hot and turn at once onto a buttered tin. Allow to cool and set and then break into pieces.

Acacia Blossom Soufflé

Soufflé à la fleur d'acacia

For four people
Preparation time: 30 minutes
Cooking time: 18 minutes

Ingredients   100 g (3½ oz) sprays of acacia blossom
caster sugar
1 tablespoon cognac
a nut of butter
6 tablespoons crème pâtissière (page 288)
5 egg whites
a pinch of salt
2 egg yolks
icing sugar

Two hours in advance

1 Set aside two clusters of acacia blossom and detach the flowers one by one from the rest, taking care not to lose the petals. When you have 50 g (1¾ oz) flowers, dust them with sugar, sprinkle on the cognac and leave them to marinate for about 2 hours.

Preparation and cooking

2 Butter the inside of a soufflé dish or a silver timbale. Put in 15 g (½ oz) caster sugar and shake the dish to coat the inside, turning the dish upside down to shake out any excess. Keep in a cool place.

3 Prepare the crème pâtissière and keep warm.

4 Take a copper basin, rub it with salt and vinegar, rinse under running water and then dry with a spotlessly clean tea towel. Put the 5 egg whites into the basin with a pinch of salt and, using a wire whisk, whisk them up, starting slowly and gradually increasing the speed. When the whites are firm and can be gathered into a single mass with the whisk, wind them up – that is, turn the whisk slowly with a circular movement which will make them thoroughly smooth.

5 Preheat the oven to 180°C/350°F/Mark 4. Add the 2 egg yolks to the crème pâtissière, whisk and heat gently. Take a quarter of the whites and mix them in, then pour this mixture into the basin and fold in the rest of the whites with a wooden spatula. Carefully stir in the acacia flowers and cognac. Turn the mixture into the soufflé dish, smooth the surface with the spatula and decorate with the two reserved clusters of blossom.

6 Leave the soufflé for a few seconds on a very hot baking sheet and then cook in the oven for 17 minutes. Sprinkle with icing sugar and serve straight away.

Crème Pâtissière for Sweet Soufflés

Crème pâtissière pour soufflés

For four people
Preparation time: 20 minutes

Ingredients   250 ml (scant half pint) milk
2 eggs
100 g (3½ oz) caster sugar
40 g (1½ oz) flour

1   Pour the milk into a small saucepan and bring to the boil. Put the whole eggs, sugar and flour into a bowl and mix well with a whisk. Gradually pour on the boiling milk in a thin stream and whisk in.

2   Pour the mixture back into the saucepan and bring to the boil, whisking to prevent the cream sticking at the bottom of the pan, and cook for 2 to 3 minutes.

3   Strain through a fine sieve into a bowl and keep warm until you are ready to use it.